Organic Coffee

This series of publications on Africa, Latin America, Southeast Asia, and Global and Comparative Studies is designed to present significant research, translation, and opinion to area specialists and to a wide community of persons interested in world affairs. The editor seeks manuscripts of quality on any subject and can usually make a decision regarding publication within three months of receipt of the original work. Production methods generally permit a work to appear within one year of acceptance. The editor works closely with authors to produce a high-quality book. The series appears in a paperback format and is distributed worldwide. For more information, contact the executive editor at Ohio University Press, 19 Circle Drive, The Ridges, Athens, Ohio 45701.

Executive editor: Gillian Berchowitz
AREA CONSULTANTS
Africa: Diane M. Ciekawy
Latin America: Thomas Walker
Southeast Asia: William H. Frederick

The Ohio University Research in International Studies series is published for the Center for International Studies by Ohio University Press. The views expressed in individual volumes are those of the authors and should not be considered to represent the policies or beliefs of the Center for International Studies, Ohio University Press, or Ohio University.

Organic Coffee
Sustainable Development by Mayan Farmers

Maria Elena Martinez-Torres

Ohio University Research in International Studies
Latin America Series No. 45
Ohio University Press
Athens

The books in the Ohio University Research in International Studies Series
are printed on acid-free paper ⊗™

Library of Congress Cataloging-in-Publication Data

Martinez-Torres, Maria Elena.
   Organic coffee : sustainable development by Mayan farmers / Maria Elena
Martinez-Torres.
      p. cm. — (Ohio University research in international studies. Latin America
series ; no. 45)
   Includes bibliographical references and index.
   ISBN-13: 978-0-89680-247-6 (pbk. : alk. paper)
   ISBN-10: 0-89680-247-7 (pbk. : alk. paper)
   1. Coffee industry—Mexico—Chiapas.   2. Coffee growers—Mexico—Chia-
pas.   3. Organic farming—Mexico—Chiapas.   I. Title.   II. Research in inte
national studies. Latin America series ; no. 45.
   HD9199.M63C475   2006
   338.1'7373097275—dc22

                                                                    20060059

*A las campesinas y los campesinos indígenas
que con su vida y su muerte son la fuente de la lucha, la resistencia,
y la esperanza.*

*To my dear compañero del alma and our son,
sharing life with you is a constant source of inspiration.*

*To all my extended family and friends,
que desarrollaron la confianza en la unidad a pesar de la adversidad.*

*To Lee Kyung Hae,
whose brave self-immolation in defense of the rural way of life left a mark
in our hearts and minds.*

Contents

Illustrations

Figures

Maps

Tables

Acknowledgments

This book would not have been possible without the help of the people of Chiapas. My warmest thanks go out to the families I interviewed for this book and their organization's staff and technicians. All were truly wonderful, and I dedicate this book to them. Muchas gracias!

The content is largely based on my Ph.D. dissertation at the University of California, Berkeley (Martinez-Torres 2003), and I want to recognize the role of the members of my committee, Laura Enríquez, Miguel Altieri, Claudia Carr, and Jonathan Fox, whose seminars, comments, and discussions provided me with stimulating insights. Their constructive feedback at all stages of the research and writing process made this endeavor possible. Their constant encouragement helped keep me on track throughout my doctoral program. I give thanks to all of them for their commitment as professors and as academic advisors.

I thank all my teachers and professors in Mexico who planted in me the seeds of knowledge committed to a better world. I want to give special recognition to my professor at UNAM, Tobyanne Beremberg, whose incisive political analysis guided my career as a geographer. I also want to thank the faculty, staff, and students at the Center for Latin American Studies and at International and Area Studies, both at UC Berkeley, for their support during my years in the program. The institutional assistance I received from the Programa de Investigaciones Multidisciplinarias sobre Mesoamérica–UNAM and the Centro de Investigaciones de Estudios Superiores en Antropología Social, both in Chiapas, were crucial in the final stages of the writing. Thanks to Alejandro Flamenco and Diego Díaz from the GIS laboratory at El Colegio de la Frontera Sur for their help in preparing the maps in this book.

Thanks to all the generous people who assisted me in this project: Cynthia Connell, Jill Harrison, Cecilia Limon, Tracy Lingo, Shaw San Liu, Mireya López, Alfonso Martínez, María del Pilar Martínez, Kevin Nugent, Juana María Ruiz Ortiz, Josue Ramírez, Samantha Rogers, Luz Sanchez, Ofelia Santis, and Mauriza Schainker. To all of you, thank you for making this research a beautiful experience of team work! I thank my brother Eduardo who introduced me to the coffee world in Chiapas and has been my constant advisor. Special thanks go to Michael Z. Jody, Hannelore Rosset, Peter Rosset, and my editors at Ohio University Press for their help with editing my less than perfect English. I have learned so much from all of them!

I give special thanks to George Collier, whose insights into the Tzotzil world helped shape my inquiries in the highlands of Chiapas, and to Jane Collier, whose comments in reshaping this book were fundamental. I also thank Eduardo Sevilla Guzmán for his cheerful feedback, bibliography, and support.

Undertaking this project would not have been possible without the unflagging support and trust of my husband, Peter Rosset. His commitment for a better world, intelligence, and love were the fuel throughout my years of challenges in graduate school. I also thank our son, Mario Rosset-Martínez, for his understanding and his help with the fieldwork. I thank them both for their patience and for their constant support in this long project.

Finally, I thank my extended Mexican family, which gave me roots in the soil of Mexico and whose love and support made me the person I am. My parents' strength and confidence in the midst of difficult situations in the transition from a rural to an urban landscape, has always been an example for all those whose lives they touched. Special thanks go to my sister Isabel, whose intense curiosity and creativity guided our young inquiries and brought books into our home.

The research for this book was funded in part by the North-South Center and by two Tinker Summer Travel Grants. Fellowships from the Mexican Consejo Nacional de Ciencia y Technologia, the Ford and MacArthur Foundations, and UC Berkeley allowed me to begin graduate studies at Berkeley.

Abbreviations

ATO	alternative trade organization
CEC	North American Commission for Environmental Cooperation
CEPCO	Coordinadora Estatal de Productores de Café de Oaxaca (Coordinating Committee of Oaxacan Coffee Producers)
CIOAC	Central Independiente de Obreros Agrícolas y Campesinos (Independent Central Body of Farmworkers and Peasants)
CNC	Confederación Nacional Campesina (National Peasant Confederation)
CNOC	Coordinadora Nacional de Organizaciones Cafetaleras (National Coordinating Committee for Coffee-Producing Organizations)
EZLN	Ejército Zapatista de Liberación Nacional (Zapatista National Liberation Army)
ha	hectare
ICA	International Coffee Agreement
ICO	International Coffee Organization
IFOAM	International Federation of Organic Agriculture Movements
INI	Instituto Nacional Indigenista (National Indigenous Institute)
INMECAFE	Instituto Mexicano del Café (Mexican Coffee Institute)
ISMAM	Indígenas de la Sierra Madre de Motozintla "San Isidro Labrador" (Union of Coffee Producers)

Lázaro Cárdenas	Unión de Ejidos "Lázaro Cárdenas" (Union of Coffee Producers)
Majomut	Unión de Ejidos del Beneficio Majomut (Union of Coffee Producers)
NGO	nongovernmental organization
OCIA	Organic Crop Improvement Association
PIDER	Programa de Inversión para el Desarrollo Rural (Mexico's Rural Development Investment Program)
PRI	Partido Revolucionario Institucional (Institutional Revolutionary Party)
La Selva	Unión de Ejidos de la Selva (Union of Coffee Producers)
TCO	Trabajo Común Organizado (organized teamwork)
UCIRI	Unión de Comunidades Indígenas de la Región del Istmo (Union of Indigenous Communities)
UE	Unión de Ejidos (union of coffee producers with "ejido" land)
UEPC	Unidad Económica de Producción y Comercialización (Economic Union for Production and Marketing)
UNAM	Universidad Nacional Autónoma de México (National Autonomous University of Mexico)
UNCAFESUR	Unión de Productores de Café de la Frontera Sur (Union of Coffee Producers)
UNORCA	Unión Nacional de Organizaciones Regionales Campesinas Autónomas (National Union of Regional Autonomous Organizations of Peasant Women)
UPCV	Unión de Productores de Café de Veracruz (Union of Coffee Producers)
UUE	Unión de Uniones de Ejidos (Union of Cooperatives)

Introduction

Understanding the Organic Coffee Boom in Chiapas

- solutions to poverty &
enviro. recovery

ALTHOUGH DECADES—if not centuries—of economic policies have en-
trenched poverty and environmental decline throughout rural areas of
Mexico and Latin America, small-scale coffee growers of mostly Mayan
origin in Chiapas, the southernmost state in Mexico, have been organizing
themselves in search of new options to confront this stark reality. Their
organizations not only may be paving the way toward alternative solutions
to widespread rural poverty but also may be generating environmental recovery based on the frequent use of organic production practices. Despite
the severe crisis that rural Mexico has undergone over the past two
decades—which came to the world's attention with the Zapatista uprising
in 1994—these peasant farmers, or *campesinos,* have converted Mexico
into the world leader in production of organic coffee.

The most important growers of organic coffee in the global economy,
mostly indigenous peasants from the mountains across the poor southern
Mexican states of Chiapas and Oaxaca, became the most organized sector
of Mexico's revitalized peasant movement in the 1980s and 1990s. As part
of the new movement, some groups (re)organized themselves into coffee
cooperatives, combining traditional communal structures with elements
of cooperative commercial enterprises. Some of them have been so successful that they provide a unique opportunity to analyze the elements that
might be involved in more sustainable rural development policies and
organization-building strategies for the future.

1

Coffee is the commercial crop best suited to the thin soils of the forested mountains in Chiapas. Coffee is also unique among Third World export crops in that most of the production and processing technologies involved were developed in producing countries. Coffee has thus contributed greatly to state formation over more than a century and to the development of modern infrastructure, since the use of nonimported technologies allowed for far more capital accumulation within producing countries than did other export crops. Today coffee, produced by both large and small farmers, continues to be an important source of foreign exchange for many countries. But recent years have seen the drastic reconfiguration of national and international coffee markets. While many of the changes hurt small-scale farmers, they simultaneously have generated new opportunities for those peasants who produce high-quality coffee—especially those who produce organically—and thus many peasant coffee cooperatives have entered the growing market segments created by the differentiation of the once monolithic coffee market into *specialty* and *gourmet* markets. Small-scale farmers have proven able to take advantage of these new market opportunities, but only when they are well organized and produce a quality product.

The organization and networking of small-scale farmers—the level of *social capital* they have built—is the key element that allows them to tap into market opportunities and to intensify their production in a sustainable manner. In rural Mexico social capital grew extensively over the last few decades through a series of iterative cycles in which both the state and civil society played central roles. Once farmers were well organized, they were able to make productive investments in the *natural capital* they possessed—land well suited for growing coffee, water, and accompanying biodiversity—via organic farming practices, and thus tap into organic coffee markets.

The formation of social capital, combined with strategies based on investments in natural capital, results in positive synergisms that lead to broad-based, sustainable development. Development that is sustainable should not be exclusionary but rather should minimize social polarization and provide opportunities for the poor to make a decent living in ways that do not degrade long-term productive resources like soil.

The level of community organization and the degree of development of local institutions play a key role in the success of development efforts. In the concept of *social capital*, social relationships are seen as resources that help people act effectively. Rural people are able to take advantage of networks, associations, and broader forms of social organization within their livelihood strategies, in order to access services, reduce risks, acquire information, and protect themselves against predatory practices. Furthermore, the importance of social cohesion within organizations with indigenous identity harkens back to the norms and social relations that create a sense of obligation.

The phrase *natural capital,* sometimes called natural assets, is increasingly being used to describe productive resources like soil, water, forests, fisheries, genetic stocks of crops and livestock, and biodiversity; the ecological processes that link them; and the environmental services they provide. Rural people need access to the natural resources of land, water, and forests in order to construct livelihoods; without a minimal stock of natural capital a rural family farm would find it difficult to survive or maintain its productivity. Families can invest in their natural assets by, for example, incorporating organic matter into the soil to improve fertility (Boyce and Pastor 2001), but natural capital can also be depreciated by such processes as soil erosion (Pretty 1998).

While most theorists have treated social capital and natural capital separately, a few analysts affirm the two go hand in hand.

Much of this book is based on a detailed study carried out with peasant coffee producers in Chiapas looking at the critical elements involved in the ongoing small-scale farmer organic coffee boom in Chiapas (Martínez-Torres 2003). The research methodology employed in the study was based on a socioeconomic and ecological survey of small coffee farms spread across different regions of Chiapas. The survey was organized by the membership of coffee-growing families in different cooperatives and farmers' organizations and by the production technologies they employ (traditional or natural, organic, transitional, and chemical based). The survey methodology is described in detail in Martínez-Torres 2003. Based on an examination of the roles of natural capital and social capital in this example of what seems to be more sustainable development, this book shows that investments in both types of capital are essential. The critical elements involved in the ongoing small-farmer organic coffee boom in Chiapas are the roles of *social capital* and *natural capital* within the context of *sustainable development.*

farmers rely on social and natural capital for prosperity

Only the formation of significant social capital allowed these coffee farmers to navigate the changing terrain of the national and global coffee market in the wake of the breakup of the International Coffee Agreement (ICA) and the disappearance of the Mexican Coffee Institute (INME-CAFE). They were truly forced to "appropriate all the steps of the production process" (a phrase coined by Mexican peasant organizations) once INMECAFE stopped offering technical assistance, transport, and marketing. With the social capital they developed, small-scale coffee growers were then able to take advantage of the niches that opened in the global market with the collapse of the ICA. More specifically, their enormous success with, indeed the boom in, organic coffee, would have been impossible without a substantial previous buildup of social capital.

What the data demonstrate most clearly, however, is how *investments* in natural assets—via conversion to organic production, the introduction of shade biodiversity, and the buildup of leaf litter and humus—have paid off in both productive (yield) and economic (gross income) terms, and in terms of ecological indicators of the future sustainability of production (erosion prevention, future soil fertility, etc.). Although mainstream critics claim that organic farming leads to low productivity, this study suggests that the opposite is true. The strategy of investment in natural capital by organic farming is a viable alternative to chemicals in terms of the intensification of coffee agriculture. Investment in natural capital has given small-scale farmers the higher prices that come from organic certification—thus helping them weather the recurrent crises of the coffee market—while maintaining soil quality for future production.

In comparison to conventional approaches to rural development, the concept of sustainable development is not only more equitable and more ecologically sound—in the sense both of not damaging the external environment and of conserving or enhancing the resource base for future production—but is economically viable for the poor. While in the larger sense the term *socially just* may mean a broad distribution of the benefits of development, in the case of coffee production technologies, that term also encompasses those options that are appropriate for smaller and poorer farmers. In that context, the low investment embodied in natural technology, and the organic farming route to the intensification of production based on applying more labor to enhance natural assets, would be favored over the more capital-intensive chemical approach (especially

4

under conditions like those of much of rural Chiapas, where the opportunity cost for family labor is low).

The payoffs from investing in natural capital and the internalization of the enviromental benefits of organic farming—via organic certification and price premiums—would be impossible to obtain without the earlier formation of significant social capital. This is partially because only effective organizations are able to obtain and maintain certification in the organic market. Furthermore, given the amount of technical assistance provided by these organizations to the farmers who are undergoing the transition to organic production, by either professional staff or by campesino-promoters, and the organizational learning involved, it is unlikely that even the natural capital investment of converting to organic could have been undertaken without having had sufficient social capital already in place. The conclusion is that in this case both forms of capital had to be cultivated in order to maximize the success of sustainable development.

The present dedication to organic coffee among small-farmer organizations in Chiapas can be seen as providing alternatives to poverty and to environmental degradation.

- environmental and economic = positive outcomes

- social networks required for success as an organic coffee farmers.

Chapter 1

The Spread of Coffee

WHILE THE COFFEE plant itself is native to the province of Kaffa in Ethiopia, coffee cultivation now spans all tropical corners of the world and, over time, has touched many aspects of global life. At some point around the year AD 700 (Pendergrast 1999, 8), the coffee plant—later classified by Carl von Linnaeus as part of the Rubiaceae family and *Coffea* genus—spread from Ethiopia to the Arabian peninsula and Egypt, where for centuries coffee was used as a medicine. The Arab physician Avicenna first recorded the medicinal use of coffee around the year AD 1000, and named the brew 'bunc.' This word for coffee is still used in Ethiopia today. There is also a popular story from AD 1400 about a shepherd who noticed his goats becoming excited after eating the berries from a particular bush. He mentioned this observation to a monk, who in turn boiled the berries and distilled from them a brew that would keep one from falling asleep.

Coffee was first cultivated commercially in Yemen, where beans were parched before export in order to destroy their ability to germinate, thus maintaining an Arab monopoly on coffee (Ukers 1935, 1–6). The main port where coffee was traded was Mocha (al-Mukhā). During the sixteenth century coffee became a popular social drink in Arabia and Persia, and it was first sold in Europe late in the same century. Coffee joined salt, sugar, tea, and spices as luxury goods in Europe during the seventeenth century. Coffee was heavily taxed, and the high price motivated European trading companies to transplant coffee to their tropical colonies.

historicizing coffee!

In 1706, a *Coffea arabica* bush was taken to the botanical garden in Amsterdam, where it became the source of seeds for the botanical garden in Paris and for the global expansion of coffee (Carvajal 1984, 13). The Dutch East Indies Company set up production in Java, Sumatra, Timor, and Ceylon; the British East India Company in India and later in Jamaica; the French Company of the Indies in Madagascar, Indochina, and French Colonial Africa. Germans introduced coffee in German East Africa, and the Belgians in the Congo (Williams 1994, 16). In all these areas, native populations were forced to work on large colonial coffee plantations as indentured labor or as slaves. "At the conquest, all lands were declared royal, and the king granted lands (and populations) to finance the conquest. Shortly thereafter, royal lands were granted as an inducement to colonization" (42).

During the Industrial Revolution, when the steam engine was adapted to ocean travel, new monopolies gained control over long-distance shipping and importing (Wolf 1982). Thus was the Arab monopoly on coffee broken, and the lower cost of shipping former luxury goods turned them into staples of the European working-class diet. The demand for coffee exploded once industrial employers realized that workers were more productive after a coffee break (Williams 1994, 17) (see figure 1.1).

boom connected to the industrial revolution

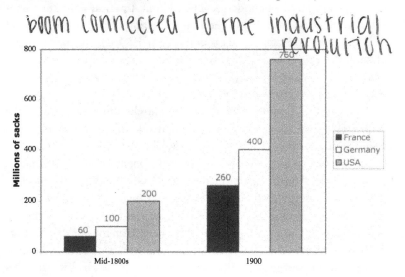

Figure 1.1. Coffee demand in France, Germany, and the United States, 1800–1900.　　　　　　　　*Source:* Williams 1994, 17–18

The first coffee-producing areas in the Americas were the islands of the Antilles, which had easy access to the Atlantic trade route. In 1715 and 1716 the French introduced coffee plants to their Caribbean colonies from Mocha (Williams 1994, 20). They began on the Bourbon Island and then in Martinique, and from there coffee expanded to the rest of the New World (Pendergrast 1999). The Portuguese introduced coffee in Brazil in 1732, and the Spanish introduced it in Cuba and Puerto Rico in 1748 and 1755, respectively. By 1784, Venezuela, with good access to the Atlantic trade route and more land area suitable for coffee cultivation, was a key supplier of the increasing demand for coffee; a century later, Brazil became the world's most important producer of coffee (Williams 1994, 20).

Ideal growing conditions were found in areas of recent volcanic activity and in older mountainous zones where deposits of organic matter had accumulated, as in Central America's Central Cordillera and in the Soconusco mountains in Chiapas, Mexico, where coffee production increased until the early part of the nineteenth century (Martinez 1997). Since establishing a coffee grove requires a huge initial investment and a wait of a few years for the first harvest, potential coffee growers were reluctant to risk investing in coffee unless they had secure, well-defined, private claims to land (Williams 1994, 41). Yet even long-standing haciendas lacked clearly defined boundaries. The Central American coffee boom resulted in demands that led to the transformation of traditional forms of land tenure into privately titled properties (42). Fueled by the privatization of land, by 1880 coffee had become the main export of the newly independent economies of Central America and Mexico (Paige 1998; Roseberry, Gudmindson, and Samper 1995).

Today, coffee is grown throughout the mid-elevation mountains of the tropics (see map 1.1), and is second only to petroleum in international trade, with a volume of 112 million sixty-kilo bags a year (ICO 2005a). Coffee is a key source of foreign exchange for many countries (see figure 1.2), such as Ethiopia with 65 percent of its GNP and 25 percent of its population engaged in the coffee sector (Gorman 1999). Coffee is produced in fifty-six countries (ICO 2005a), covering more than 10 million hectares and involving some 25 million coffee farmers worldwide (Rice 2003, 230). Currently, the world's most important coffee producer is Brazil, with an average of 35 million bags a year, followed by Vietnam (12.5 million), Colombia (11 million), Indonesia (6.5 million), India (4.8 million), and Mexico (4.7 million). The Latin American countries produce almost 50 percent of the world's coffee (FNC 2005).

Recall that the production and processing technologies involved in coffee were mostly developed in the producing countries themselves,

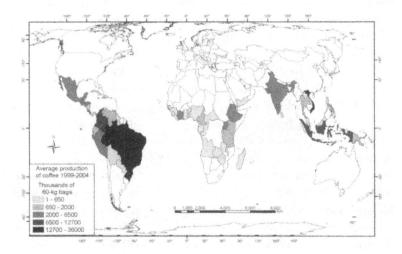

Map 1.1. Worldwide distribution of coffee

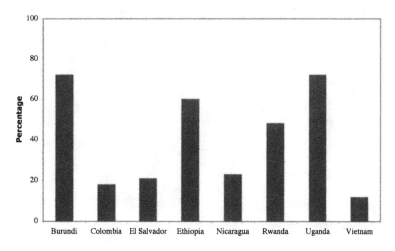

Figure 1.2. Relative export earnings from coffee.

Source: Dicum and Luttinger 1999

9

rather than having been imported from industrialized countries, as has been the case for other commodities like cotton (Williams 1994, 106). This characteristic contributed greatly to historical state formation and to the development of modern infrastructure in many southern nations (246), since the use of domestic technology allowed for far more capital accumulation inside producing countries compared to other export crops for which a good part of the foreign exchange earned went to pay for imported technology.

Coffee was introduced to Mexico in 1795 when Juan Antonio Gómez de Guevara planted seeds brought from Havana on the Hacienda de Guadalupe in Córdoba, Veracruz (Escamilla 1993). Coffee plantations proliferated during Spanish colonial rule as a way for *hacendados* to claim land from the viceroy. By 1802, 209 sixty-kilo bags were exported, and three years later, 257 (Martinez 1997, 18). Coffee was first introduced to the Soconusco region in Chiapas in the mid-nineteenth century (Catalán 1995; Renard 1993; Villafuerte and Meza 1993). During the first decades of Mexico's independent period, coffee was produced on plantations in the states of Chiapas, Veracruz, Colima, Oaxaca, Michoacán, and Morelos. Throughout the rest of the century, the crop spread to the rest of today's coffee-producing states, Guerrero, Hidalgo, Jalisco, Nayarit, Puebla, San Luis Potosí, and Tabasco (see map 1.2). Coffee prices rose thanks to grow-

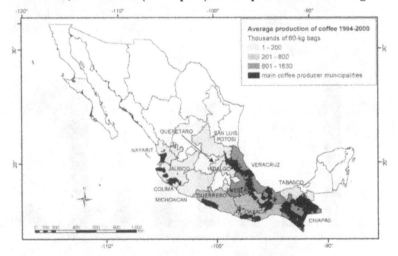

Map 1.2. Coffee-producing regions of Mexico

ing demand from the United States, and between 1888 and 1897 production increased from 80,000 to 400,000 sixty-kilo bags. This marked the emergence of Mexico as a major coffee-exporting country (Nolasco 1985, 169–70).

Coffee, like other export crops, was cultivated exclusively on large plantations, on which workers were severely mistreated, until 1910, when the Mexican revolution marked the start of a gradual process of the breakup of the largest estates. The agrarian reform process distributed marginal land to thousands of rural families in a collective form of property called the *ejido,* and recognized the communal land rights of indigenous communities across Mexico. The mixed planting of corn, squash, and beans, with the raising of small animals like chickens, helped these rural families survive despite their exclusion from the modernization process occurring in many parts of the country.

Among them were former hacienda workers who brought coffee trees to their land mainly as ornamentals. Those whose land was more suitable for coffee—land considered marginal for most other commercial crops (Wohlgemuth 1996)—were motivated to plant coffee as a cash crop when prices were particularly high after World War I. In 1958 the Mexican Coffee Institute (INMECAFE) was established to disseminate technological innovations and to expand coffee production. Marketing was still done by private companies, but Mexican federal government support programs targeted incentives for coffee production (Nolasco 1985, 82). The rise in coffee prices pushed the largest expansion of the area planted up to fifty thousand hectares in 1970, and to seventy-nine thousand in 1986 (Catalan 1995).

Coffee soon became one of the most important export commodities for Mexico. In the late twentieth century, coffee was the second most important source of foreign currency, after petroleum (Martínez 1997), with a peak annual value of US$900 million in 1997. Although the average annual production has been 230,000 tons over the last twelve years, there have been huge differences in the prices received (see figure 1.3). This is a direct result of the new volatility of prices after the reconfiguration of the international coffee market during the 1990s (as detailed in chapter 3). Since 1998 there has been a tendency for coffee prices to fall, which has placed coffee in a less prominent position among Mexican exports. Nevertheless, tens of thousands of families depend on the coffee economy for their livelihoods.

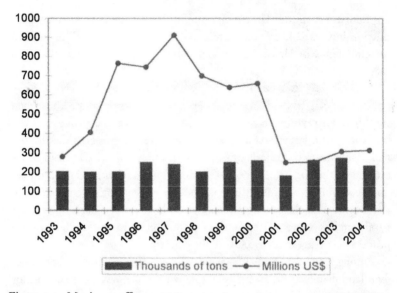

Figure 1.3. Mexican coffee exports.   *Sources:* Bancomex 2002, 1, and ICO 2005

In today's Mexico, there are still many large coffee plantations, but the majority of Mexican coffee producers are small farmers. In fact, 92 percent of Mexican producers have between one and five hectares of coffee (see table 1.1). There are almost three hundred thousand coffee farms in Mexico (Harvey 1994; Plaza, Contreras, and Bray 1998), which occupy approximately eight hundred thousand hectares and employ some two million people (Celis, Ejea, and Hernández 1991). For rural Mexicans, coffee is their second most important source of income, following the remittances that expatriate migrant workers send to their families.

Mexico City, Comitán, Córdoba, Jalapa, and Tapachula are the five main commercial centers of the coffee industry in Mexico, and two of them are located in Chiapas. Chiapas produces more coffee than any other Mexican state, accounting for 37 percent of national production, and making coffee the state's most important cash crop (COPLADE, 2000). From the Soconusco, in the southeastern part of the state, coffee spread to the sierra, the northern region, the highlands, and, finally, the jungle region. Today, coffee is grown mainly by small farmers in practically all regions of Chiapas that are suitable for coffee production.

TABLE 1.1
Size of coffee producers in Mexico in 1992

Plot size (ha)	Number of producers	Percentage of total
0–2	194,538	68.91
2–5	64,377	22.80
5–10	17,881	6.33
10–20	4,291	1.52
20–50	808	0.29
50–100	246	0.09
100–150	178	0.06
Total	282,319	100

Source: Harvey 1994

Dual or even multiple economies share the same geographical space in the coffee regions of Mexico. The subsistence peasant economy, with some commercial production oriented toward the internal market, co-exists alongside an agricultural export economy, and coffee is present in both of them. This mix of large and small, rich and poor, generates a rich cultural, social, and economic diversity, with a broad range of technologies employed (Perez Brignoli and Samper 1994).

- coffee farming now = small-scale

produced across
ses

Chapter 2

How Coffee Is Produced

THE COFFEE WE consumers drink is produced in three phases: cultivation, processing, and roasting. In the first phase, selected coffee seeds are germinated and kept in covered nurseries. Two months later, coffee seedlings are put in small pots or plastic bags filled with soil prepared with fertilizer. More mature seedlings are transplanted to the field four months later. The genus *Coffea* contains some eighty species; however, only two species are typically cultivated around the world: *C. arabica*—accounting for three-quarters of the world's coffee production—and *C. canephora*, also known as robusta (Carvajal 184, 13). *C. arabica* is characterized by its self-fertilization (with pollen from the same flower) (14), and is the main species grown in Chiapas.

Cultivation in the steeply sloped terrain of Chiapas involves clearing, burning, plowing, and hole digging before planting. Escamilla (1993) reports that the most common planting design used in Mexico is a symmetric one, either square or rectangular, depending on the distances between plants within a row and between rows (imagine connecting four neighboring coffee plants, to see if the lines form a square or a rectangle). Usually only some of the more intensive producers use an asymmetric design, with contours along the slopes. Once a coffee grove is established, labor is needed throughout the year for fertilization, weeding, pruning, disease control, harvesting, and replanting, and also for pruning the shade trees, if these are part of the design. Fertilizers are often used to replenish nitrogen, potassium, and calcium and, to a lesser degree, phosphorous and magnesium. Weeds are of particular concern for newly planted coffee groves, and weeding is one of the most common cultivation practices in coffee-producing areas.

As the coffee plant grows, pruning keeps it within a manageable height and gives form to the new branches, so that they will produce more berries and facilitate harvesting. There are almost as many different pruning techniques as there are coffee producers, because their farms are distributed over so many different soil types and environments (Rice 1993). Nevertheless, the most common category of pruning techniques in Latin America is that of individual pruning (in Mexico known as *Veracruzana*), in which each plant is pruned as needed. The pruning of shade trees is also important, to maintain the proper balance of shade, sunlight, and air flow for the growing coffee plants.

Coffee requires a moderate amount of patchy shade to produce optimum yields, because coffee leaves photosynthesize less when exposed to a lot of direct sunlight (Carbajal 1984, 17–20). The ideal shade trees not only help maintain soil fertility, but also offer a branch and foliar structure that promotes beneficial air circulation in the coffee grove. In the early 1980s INMECAFE recommended that all natural shade trees be replaced with nitrogen-fixing leguminous shade trees primarily from the *Inga* genus. (For the species used in Chiapas, see table 2.1). There is a growing body of literature written about, and research being carried out on, the many benefits that shade brings to the whole production system and its associated environment. Shade canopies create habitats for migratory birds, as well

TABLE 2.1
Shade trees used in Chiapas coffee regions

Common Name	Scientific Name	Region
Chalum	*Inga micheliana* Harms	Sierra, Soconusco, highlands
Paterna	*Inga paterno* Harms	Las Margaritas, highlands
Tzelel	*Inga punctata* Wild	highlands, north
Chalum Colorado	*Inga rodrigueziana* Pitt	

Source: Soto 2001; author's fieldwork

as producing 107 useful, harvestable products in and of themselves (Greenberg 1996; Greenberg, Bichier, Cruz, and Retsma 1997; Mas and Dietsch 2000; Nestel and Altieri 1992; Perfecto, Rice, Greenberg, and Van der Voort 1996; Perfecto and Vandermeer 1994; Rice, 2000; Rice and Ward 1996). Farmers also benefit from the reduction of labor needs, as many weeds are shaded out, or blocked by leaf litter:

Antes sí tenemos que limpiar su café, ahorita ya hay sombra, ya no necesita de limpiar con azadón, hay veces, si trabajan con azadón, pero ahorita ya no porque su parcela, su cafetal ya tiene sombra, ya no tiene mucho pasto.

[Before, yes, we had to weed the coffee, but now it has shade, now we don't need to hoe any more, except once in a great while. The coffee grove has shade now, so it has very few weeds.]

Marisol Gutiérrez, tzotzil organic farmer from Poconichim, eastern highlands[1]

After the coffee tree reaches about five years of age, depending on the coffee species and environmental conditions, the coffee berries are harvested for the first time, and every year thereafter. The duration of the harvest period varies according to the microclimate of each coffee plot. In some places the harvest is concentrated within a month or less; in others it can last for up to four months. In the different regions of Chiapas the harvest season begins in November at lower altitudes and ends in late March at higher elevations. Although a mature coffee plant can produce for up to thirty years, its productive life starts declining after ten years in production, and after fifteen it is considered to be an old plant that produces only with extra pruning (Nolasco 1985, 112).

Each step of the production process, from cultivation through roasting, may vary in accordance with the details of the local farming practices used, as well as with such other factors as scale, the processing technologies available locally, and the target market.

Coffee Cultivation Technologies

Coffee farmers use one or a combination of three principal techniques of coffee cultivation: (1) natural, also called traditional or sometimes passive organic; (2) intensive chemical, also called technified or conventional or just chemical; and (3) intensive organic, also called certified organic or just organic.

NATURAL CULTIVATION

Until recently the only common method of coffee cultivation by small-scale farmers in Mexico (with many regional variations) was the traditional, shade-grown method, which is also known as passive organic cultivation but which I will refer to as natural. Natural producers take the seedlings that emerge on their own in their fields and randomly plant them using holes that are relatively small, under a diverse multilayered canopy of natural shade trees. Traditional or natural technology is the province of those small-scale producers who devote minimum labor and investment to their coffee groves. Generally, natural producers do not fertilize at all, relying on the slow process of natural regeneration of soil fertility, although a very small number of them use chemical fertilizers on rare occasions for a quick boost in productivity. The Guatemalan technique of pruning known as *agobio* is quite common among traditional producers in Chiapas, and entails bending the plant so that new branches will grow upwards. The flowers and berries appear one year after a branch has received this treatment; once these branches have produced, they do not produce again and are trimmed off. *Agobio* is performed every two years (Escamilla 1993).

The vegetative structure of a traditional or natural coffee farm is forest-like. The shade species may include legumes—trees of the *Inga* family—fruit trees, banana plants, and hardwood. In natural and organic groves weeding is done by hand, using a machete. However, coffee groves in which a high percentage of soil is covered with leaf litter—as is typically the case in natural and organic groves—do not have weeds, and therefore save the producer labor or money, or both. The presence of all these tree species creates a stable production system, and they yield useful products for the farmers. Shade also provides protection from erosion and constantly replenishes the soil through the decomposition of leaf litter and other organic matter. Favorable temperature and humidity are also maintained (Martínez and Peters 1991; 1994), and an array of beneficial insects is supported that keep potential pests under control (Perfecto and Vandermeer 1994). Traditional coffee is considered the most ecologically sound

17

agro-forestry system in Mesoamerica (Rice 1993, 2000; Perfecto, Rice, Greenberg, and Van der Voort 1996).

Basically there are two ways to boost—or "intensify"—production on traditional coffee farms, and these yield the two other production techniques. One is to implement intensive organic farming practices, and the other is to use farm chemicals.

INTENSIVE CHEMICAL CULTIVATION

The Green Revolution came late to coffee production, but during the 1980s and early 1990s Green Revolution-style *technified cultivation* spread dramatically in Latin America's large and medium-sized coffee plantations, as well as to other parts of the world (Rice 1993; Richter 1993). This so-called modernization of the production process consists of the use of high-yield varieties of seeds, agrochemical inputs, and the significant reduction, or outright elimination, of shade (Rice 1999, 568).

To convert a coffee grove to this method, typically the coffee plants and the shade trees are partially or completely removed, and the coffee is replaced with new sun-tolerant coffee hybrids planted in open rows[2] along the slope, while the use of purchased chemical inputs like fertilizer, herbicide, and fungicide is initiated or intensified (566). *Technification, renovation, rehabilitation, revitalization,* and *technology transfer* are among the terms that have been used to describe this method of cultivation.

Technification has generally introduced low stature, compact varieties of *Coffea arabica*. The most common variety is *caturra*, a mutant dwarf variety discovered in Brazil in the last century, which yields its first crop in the third year—almost two years earlier than the traditional varieties of *típica* or *borbón* (Rice 1993). A hybrid known as *arabusta*, a cross between *C. arabica* and *C. canephora*, developed in Timor, was also introduced because of its resistance to rust fungus. Planting densities typically change from 2 m between plants in traditional cultivation to just 35 to 40 cm on the densely planted technified plantations.

The new varieties respond well to chemical inputs such as fertilizer, and are relatively sun tolerant. But without shade, weeds proliferate, so the new systems require intensive use of herbicides or manual labor (or both). Part of this heavy use of agrochemicals has been a product of loan requirements, in which growers had to agree to purchase specific chemical inputs in order to get bank credit for technified production (Nolasco 1985). With technification, coffee went from being an exception among export crops for its low reliance on imported chemical inputs, to a more typical export crop that, like cotton and bananas before it, now depends heavily on agrochemicals.

The productive life of each plant in this system is only six to seven years (Arenas Melo 1981). It is as though the plant is exhausted by the constant "pumping through" of synthetic nutrients used in chemical production systems. These systems require much more frequent replanting, which greatly raises long-term production costs. Technified coffee uses a simplified pruning or "stumping back" system, in which the main stems of five- or six-year-old plants are chopped off some 40 cm above the ground.

Technified farming does not require that the farmer have any detailed knowledge of plant growth and ecology in particular microhabitats, because it is based on a one-size-fits-all cookbook technology. Only large and medium coffee producers have fully adopted this intensive technology in Chiapas, and they are not the subject of this book. However, many small-scale producers have adopted part of the technification package, like agrochemicals for fertilization and weeding, and they have also reduced (though not eliminated) their shade, and may or may not have replaced their coffee varieties. This somewhat technified combination of natural technology with the use of chemical fertilizers or pesticides is known as "conventional" technology among producers, and I will call it *chemical technology*. While this type of chemical intensification is environmentally destructive, organic, like natural cultivation, is considered a stable and ecologically sound agroforestry system.

INTENSIVE ORGANIC CULTIVATION

Organic cultivation in Chiapas is an intensive form of traditional farming that is based on a detailed knowledge of the pattern of plant growth in particular environments. The main characteristic is the intensive use of labor for the care of the plant. It is similar to traditional or natural methods in that substantial shade is used, though typically the density and diversity of shade is somewhat lower than in natural cultivation. Organic cultivation also resembles technified production in that there is more intensive use of inputs, although organic inputs and human labor are substituted for the agrochemicals used in chemical methods (Sanchez 1990).

19

Organic producers have a nursery for seedling production, from which coffee plants are transplanted to square holes 40 cm wide and equally deep. The soil is prepared with enriched compost. The compost is produced from local materials, and constitutes the only fertilizer used. The main ingredients in the compost are the waste pulp yielded by coffee processing, green plant trimmings, manure, and virtually any other organic matter at hand. Some producers purchase inputs like lime and manure from off-farm sources to enrich their compost. Organic fertilization requires three kilograms of compost per coffee plant per year. On average fifty plants can be fertilized per person per day. Every region produces compost in a different way, with different costs. For example, in Kulaktic, in the eastern highlands of Chiapas, compost production requires three person-days per bin, and farmers do not purchase compost materials. In contrast, in Ojo de Agua in the upper zone of the Margaritas jungle of Chiapas, it takes six person-days per compost bin, and some farmers buy manure to use as a compost ingredient.

Nosotros estuvimos acarreando aquí pura tierra abonada para sembrar las matitas de café, hicimos unos hoyos y acarreamos pura tierra abonada. Así como es como sembramos las matas de café.

[We were hauling in compost to transplant the coffee seedlings. We'd dig holes, and fill them with compost. And that's how we planted this coffee.]

Francisca Mendez, mestiza organic farmer from Santo Domingo, Soconusco

... desde entonces cuidamos el café con abono orgánico, es importante porque la tierra ya se desgastó tanto, por tanta agua pues, tantos barrancos, ahora tenemos que cuidar porque ahora no se puede sembrar una mata así nada más, tienes que echar abono si no, no pega.

[... ever since we've fertilized this coffee with organic compost, this is important because the soil was so worn out, from so much water, so many gullies, that now we take better care of it because otherwise you can't plant anything; you use compost, otherwise nothing grows.]

Roberto Quijano, mestizo organic farmer, Rincon del Bosque, Sierra

Plant care involves a very selective pruning of the coffee plant and the shade trees. Each plant is examined to determine the specific care it needs. Intensive organic farming is the only technology in which the laborious work of carefully selecting the branches that are going to be cut is done twice (a first and second thinning). Pruning boosts berry production on the plant. It is critically important to exercise care in pruning the shade trees so that their branches produce a patchy pattern of shade that changes during the day. Too much shade can cause humidity problems and coffee rust fungus. Pruning back the excess branches allows greater air flow and penetration of sunlight. To regenerate an older organic coffee grove, a combination of replanting with new coffee plants and the *recepa* is used.

The construction of terraces is another unique feature of organic production and is usually performed on a plant-by-plant basis. A mini-platform of earth is built up around each plant to slow the runoff of rainwater and to promote better percolation. Terraces demand a great deal of labor, and the time required increases on steep slopes and rocky soils. Although terrace building is the usual technical recommendation to avoid excessive soil erosion in hilly areas, in forestlike coffee plantations it may not always be necessary, as leaf litter, mulch, and living barriers (tall, strong grasses or bushes planted in contour lines) can all greatly reduce erosion, and require little or no extra labor.

The final unique characteristic of organic cultivation is that to receive the price premium, the coffee groves most be certified as organic by a certifying company or organization. The International Federation of Organic Agriculture Movements (IFOAM), founded in Germany in 1972, promotes organic farming around the world, and has developed detailed agroecological requirements that producers must satisfy if their coffee is to be certified. To make the certification process more accessible to farmer organizations, IFOAM has accredited a number of local certifying organizations in different countries (Raynolds 2000, 5). In Mexico, for example, there are now several different certifying organizations, which are accredited for different export markets (the United States vs. various European countries). Often coffee producers' organizations must pay for several of these certifications, since different clients require different certifying agencies.

EACH OF THESE general categories of cultivation has specific adaptations in the different microclimates of the regions within Chiapas. Nevertheless, one can generalize about their overall features. Table 2.2 lists the important distinguishing characteristics of the three main production methods, based on a study of three farms in the Soconusco region of Chiapas.

TABLE 2.2

Characteristics of coffee cultivation, Soconusco, Chiapas

Characteristic	Natural	Organic	Technified
Biodiversity	high	high	very low
Agrochemical use	very low	none	very high
Coffee varieties	tall	tall and short	short and compact
Density	1,600 plants/ha	2,500–2,800 plants/ha	4,000–5,000 plants/ha
Planting design	contour	contour	contour or along slope
Weeding	manual	manual	herbicides
Fertilization	organic fertilizer or low dose of fertilizer (240 kg/ha, 18–12–6)	organic compost (6 tons/ha), nutrients recycled	1,000 kg/ha fertilizer (18–12–6), 1,000 kg/ha urea
Shade	multistory canopy, 10–12 species, excess shade common	multistory canopy, >40 species, regulated shade	none or low canopy (3 species of *Inga*), severely pruned
Pest control	natural	natural, manual, biological	chemical (Endosulfan, 1–2 lit/ha)
Replacement of coffee trees	~3%/yr	~10%/yr	~25%/yr
Yield	460–552 kg/ha	828–920 kg/ha	1,150–1,380 kg/ha
Recent price regime	low, unstable	high, stable	low, unstable
Investment, production costs	high initial investment, then very low production costs	high	high
Sustainability	stable yield	stable yield	not sustainable, initial high yields drop over time

Source: Martínez and Peters 1991, 1995

Harvest, Labor, and Preliminary Processing

Harvesting plays a critical role in determining the quality of the green coffee beans. It is very important to harvest only the ripe coffee berries without breaking the base of the stem, which would damage the generative tissue. Since each branch has beans in different stages of ripeness at any given moment, the harvesting of coffee plants involves examining each plant to pick only the ripe berries. This requirement has proven to be a major obstacle to the mechanization of this crop. Depending on the processing capacity of the producer, the climate, and the acreage of land planted, producers make three or four passes over each plant during an average two-month harvesting period. On the first harvesting round early ripening berries are collected and diseased or dry berries are eliminated. In the last round all the berries left on the plant are collected in order to prepare the plant for the next flowering period. Moreover, remaining berries would become foci for pest infestations. Some farmers prune their trees after the harvest and collect the last berries at that time.

LABOR

Among small-scale farmers, coffee-growing activities are mainly carried out by all members of the family, though even these farmers might hire some additional labor—two to ten people—or engage in labor exchanges at harvest time. Since harvesting requires more work than any other activity in coffee growing, the labor demand peaks at harvest time in all technological approaches (see figure 2.1). Escamilla (1993) estimates that harvest labor constitutes 40 to 60 percent of the production costs of growing coffee. The labor hired means that, compared to most of economically depressed rural Mexico, there is more work in coffee areas, though this too has been depressed during the recent years of low coffee prices.[3]

Medium-scale farmers hire from ten to seventy workers, and larger farmers from several hundred to a thousand workers. Hired labor in coffee production usually consists of seasonal migrant farm workers, who come from economically depressed surrounding areas. In the Soconusco, for example, workers from the highlands and from the north, as well as a good number of Guatemalans with a Mexican work permit similar to the U.S. *Bracero* program, work on all large coffee plantations and even on

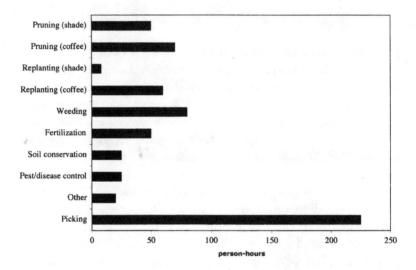

Figure 2.1. Coffee farm activities (person-hours per acre).

Source: Williams 1994, 110

small and medium-sized farms. Years ago, labor recruiters went to rural towns to find workers (Carvalho 1994). Today the workers usually have established relations with the farmers and they arrive on their own. In the case of Guatemalans they come on foot, but generally large growers pay for transportation.

Often the entire Guatemalan family comes to work on large coffee fincas in the Soconusco, with children working alongside the adult men and women.[4] The family signs a contract in which only the adults are included, and are paid piece rate. Workers bring their own bedding and live in crowded barracks in poor conditions where diseases such as tuberculosis spread easily (Freyermuth and Godfrey 1992). The workers are organized in teams, and the foreman is usually a member of the owner's family or is one of the permanent workers on the plantation. During the year, each team is assigned a task, and they are paid when the task is done, maximizing the efficiency of the labor force. During the harvest they are assigned rows to harvest. Sometimes labor contractors sign up a large farm. In this case, the owners pay them a fixed amount and the contractor finds the workers and takes care of the job without interference from the owner.

During the harvest, wages are fixed in advance by the farmers. Usually the collector uses a palm-leaf or plastic basket with a capacity of about five kilos of coffee berries, attached to the waist. Technified coffee is easy to pick because there is less other vegetation, and a higher density of plants, so workers pick more in the same amount of time. Since pay is piece rate, workers prefer to work on technified farms, which are usually larger. Thus small farms have trouble hiring labor in the Soconusco, and must offer better wages or other incentives in many cases. Because the majority of coffee labor is seasonal, organizing is difficult, and today unions are generally absent from coffee-growing regions.[5]

PROCESSING

There are two technological challenges for small-scale farmers in processing their crop: depulping the coffee berries and drying the resulting green coffee beans. Coffee berries must be depulped the same day they are picked, otherwise the quality of the coffee drops dramatically. There are two basic technologies used for removing the layers of pulp that cover the green coffee bean: the dry method which produces natural coffees, and the wet method, which produces "washed" coffees, also known as *suaves*.

Dry Method

The dry method is a low-tech method in which the berries are spread out on dirt patios. The farmers wait for the pulp to ferment and rupture the outer skin, then remove the remaining layers of the green bean manually. The drawback of this method is that the fermentation gives a sour flavor to the beans, which then bring a lower price. This method is used extensively in Brazil, Vietnam, and Africa, but only 10 to 15 percent of Mexican coffee is processed this way (Santoyo, Díaz, and Rodríguez 1994). There are no estimates of how many producers practice the dry method in the state of Chiapas, where poverty and problems of road accessibility make this process more common. All producers, however, use this method to obtain coffee for their own consumption and for all coffee picked on the very last harvesting pass.

Wet Method

The wet method is used to produce green coffee of export quality. The technologies small producers use for this method vary depending on their access to machinery. Many producers process their coffee with their own small manual depulping machine—a simple mill that can also be attached to an electric motor. But typically those farmers who live near their co-op's regional mill—if they have one—take their coffee there to be processed.

In the wet process, the berries are floated in water in order to separate the unripe from the ripe ones, and then a depulping machine separates the pulp from the beans of the ripe berries. However, because the separation of unripe berries is incomplete, organic quality standards do not allow flotation. (Any unripe berries that enter the depulping process will yield beans that are not of export quality.) Organic producers must therefore be much more selective during harvesting, in order to pick only ripe berries, which they put in the depulping machine the same day or, at the latest, the following day. The unripe beans are recycled as compost.

After depulping, the beans are still covered with a sweet, sticky film, which is then dissolved during a twenty-four-hour fermentation. Producers may use plastic sacks or small wood or concrete tanks to ferment and wash the beans. Natural producers generally use plastic sacks, but organic producers use only tanks. After the fermentation, the beans are washed again and either spread out on concrete patios to dry in the sun until they contain only 12 percent humidity. Most sun drying takes between three and fifteen days, depending on the weather. Farmers try not to exceed five days of sun drying, so that the beans do not absorb odors or flavors from the surrounding environment (Santoyo, Díaz, and Rodríguez 1994).

At this point, the dried beans are called coffee in parchment. Most producers sell their coffee in this form either to their coffee organization's mill or to a middleman. The parchment—the final layer of skin—is removed mechanically in a thresher to obtain what is called green coffee. The beans are then sorted by size and density and flawed beans are removed.

The smaller-sized beans are preferred for European consumption, while the larger sizes go to the U.S. market. Intensive quality control is necessary during processing, as either excessive variability in size or the inclusion of imperfect beans will affect the flavor after roasting. Defective beans are directed to local domestic markets, where quality standards are typically lower. Finally, green coffee is bagged in sixty-kilo sacks and, if it is organic, labeled with its origin.

Roasting and Packaging

Once the green coffee bean is produced, it must be roasted to make it drinkable. The most common roasting method is to direct hot air onto the beans using some form of natural gas or propane. During a first roasting, at about 435°F, the beans pop, almost like popcorn. The final roast has different grades related to the temperature at which the beans are roasted. Light roast is obtained at 455°, Espresso at 465°, Full City at 474°, and French roast at 485°. There is a second "pop" at 480° making a French lighter than the rest, and Turkish roast is finished at 490° (RBP 1994).

At present, coffee grown in Chiapas is usually exported to Europe or the United States, to be roasted there. However, many producer organizations are exploring the possibilities of exporting roasted coffee in order to capture more value added (a higher price). At the moment many Mexican coffee organizations are selling roasted beans on the national market with a number of successful stories, though the Mexican coffee economy depends primarily on the international green coffee market.

Chapter 3

The International Coffee Market

SINCE ITS INCEPTION, the international coffee market has been an arena of constant battles for control and regulation of a sector capable of generating tremendous revenues and power. The coffee marketing system consists of a complicated web of growers, consumers, processors, brokers, exporters, importers, roasters, wholesalers, retailers, and in each exporting country, either a governmental or a quasi-governmental institute or agency that regulates or otherwise intervenes in the market (see figure 3.1 for a generic commodity chain).

The powerful members of each node of the coffee marketing chain may perform more than one function. In a producing country, for example, some large growers handle coffee from harvest through export, while some processors handle both the processing and exporting functions. The same happens in importing countries. Wholesalers, for instance, may also import and roast coffee, and in some cases of total vertical integration, can operate retail outlets, as in the case of Starbucks. Vertical and horizontal integration of several nodes of the marketing chain that cut across both producing and importing countries is also common. Multinational corporations are the principal actors in the global coffee market, but this has not always been the case.

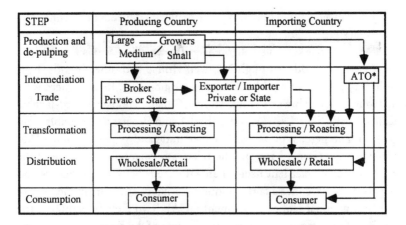

Figure 3.1. Generic coffee commodity chain.
*ATO = alternative trade organization

Historical Features of the Coffee Market

Historically, in both national and international markets, demand has de-termined how financial, material, and human resources have been allo-cated for expansion and changes in technology and quality. However, producer-country power grew within the coffee industry when the nature of production became monopsonistic. This meant that only a few coun-tries contributed to the production of more than half of the world's coffee. For many years the principal producing countries expended tremendous effort to maintain high prices in the coffee market. Brazil, for example, de-stroyed its entire harvest in 1906 to prevent coffee prices from dropping. Prices reached a high of $2.52 per pound in 1911 (Dicum and Luttinger 1999, 75), and from 1921 to 1944 Brazil burned 74 million sacks to maintain relatively high prices (Junguito and Pizano 1993). The high prices pro-vided incentives for Europeans to establish new coffee plantations in their colonies in Africa, which became important growers of *robusta* coffees (Dicum and Luttinger 1999, 81). However, during the Second World War demand for coffee dropped drastically and the competition for sales forced prices to drop as well. The downward trend continued after the war and coffee reached a low of thirty cents per pound in 1960, which severely damaged the economies of the countries dependent on coffee as a principal source of income.

The coffee market is also oligopolistic, with only a few major buyers. In 1965 General Foods, through Maxwell House and other brands, controlled 15 percent of world coffee consumption (87). In 2001 there were just four principal buyers: Philip Morris (General Foods-Suchard-Jacobs-Kraft), Nestlé, Sara Lee (Douwe Egberts), and Procter and Gamble (Folger), with 60 percent of the world coffee trade and 73 percent of the U.S. coffee market (Renard 1999). The bilaterally oligopolistic nature of the world coffee market lent itself to an agreement between producers and buyers that gave coffee a fairly unique governance structure in the form of the International Coffee Agreement (ICA). Two factors facilitated the signing of the agreement in 1963: the concern of the Kennedy administration about the possible spread of communism in poor countries if their income continued to be very low, and the inelastic U.S. demand for coffee. The ICA established production quotas for each country and stabilized prices. The International Coffee Organization was established to implement the quota system, guaranteeing each country access to the market. The agreement eventually grouped fifty producing countries (99 percent of world production) and twenty-five consuming countries (90 percent of world consumption), serving to balance the competing interests of buyers and sellers.

One of the results of the ICA was the strengthening of the governmental institutions that existed in almost all coffee-producing countries to support coffee production. In general, marketing boards prevailed in anglophone countries (Nigeria, Kenya, India). These agencies usually had a legal monopoly over the purchase of the entire coffee crop. All coffee was sold to the board, which then exported it. Agencies called *caisse de stabilization* (stabilization boards) prevailed in the francophone producing countries (Ivory Coast, Cameroon, Madagascar). These agencies established the price for private buyers and sellers, and they appropriated the difference between the higher world coffee price and the locally established one (UN 1984).

Marketing and distribution coffee institutes, quasi-governmental coffee producer associations, were common in Latin American coffee-producing areas such as Brazil, Colombia, Central America, and Mexico (see table 3.1). These powerful agencies established a guaranteed minimum price

TABLE 3.1

Coffee marketing agencies by country in 1984

Country	Agency*	Functions before liberal reform (privatization)								
		1	2	3	4	5	6	7	8	9
Brazil	IBC	x	-	x	x	-	-	x	x	-
Cameroon	ONCPB	x	-	-	x	-	-	-	x	-
Colombia	FEDERECAFE	x	x	x	x	x	x	x	x	x
Costa Rica	ICAFE	x	-	x	-	-	-	-	-	-
El Salvador	INACAFE	x	x	x	x	-	x	-	x	-
Haiti	IHPCAFE	-	x	-	-	-	-	-	-	-
India	ICB	x	-	x	x	-	x	-	x	-
Ivory Coast	CSSPPA	x	-	-	-	-	x	x	x	-
Kenya	CBK	x	-	x	-	-	x	x	x	x
Mexico	INMECAFE	x	x	-	x	-	x	x	x	x
Nicaragua	ENCAFE	x	-	-	x	-	-	-	-	-
Uganda	NCMB	-	-	-	x	-	x	-	-	-
Tanzania	TCMB	x	x	x	-	-	x	x	-	x

KEY: 1: Establishing minimum guarantee price for producers. 2: Defining domestic delivery requirements. 3: Establishing minimum export price. 4: Having direct export role. 5: Owning and managing shipping facilities. 6: Owning and managing processing facilities. 7: Investing in infrastructure. 8: Extending agricultural credit. 9: Organizing co-operatives.

Source: UN 1984, 9

* The following are the complete names of the coffee institutes or agencies listed in table 3.1, followed by the year(s) in which liberalization reforms transformed the agency or it was privatized (where available): Instituto Brasilerio do Café (IBC), 1990; Office National de Comercialisation des Produits de Base Cameroonian (ONCPB), 1992; Federación Nacional de Cafeteros de Colombia (FEDERECAFE, later FNC), 1995; Instituto del Cafe de Costa Rica (ICAFE); Instituto Nicaragüense del Café (INACAFE); Instituto Hondureño del Café (IHPCAFE); Indian Coffee Board (ICB),1992 to 1996; Caisse de Stabilisation et de Soutien des Prix de Production Agricole (CSSPPA), 1990s; Coffee Board of Kenya (CBK), 1993; Instituto Mexicano del Café (INMECAFE), 1989; Instituto Nacional de Café (INCAFE), 1989; National Coffee Marketing Board (NCMB), 1991; Tanzania Coffee Marketing Board (TCMB) 1994

and exercised a strong role in setting world prices. In some countries the institute was the only buyer, as in El Salvador and Mexico, while in others, growers could sell either to the institute or to private exporters at a free market price. A coffee institute may also have been responsible for the distribution of export quotas and the collection of the export taxes that financed the state apparatus (Williams 1994). The Mexican Coffee Institute (INMECAFE) from 1973 to 1989 was also in charge of research, technical support, subsidies, credit, storage, and distribution, becoming instrumental in bringing small-scale farmers into the world coffee market.

The ICA was in force from 1972 to 1989 and was suspended twice during those twenty-seven years.[1] Since the 1989 collapse of the orginal ICA, the New York and London futures markets have set world prices for arabicas and robustas, repectively. The ICO continued to administer a subsequent and far less powerful ICA. ICO is still the main intergovernmental organization that keeps production and trade records and agrees on rules to calculate prices. Its composite indicator price is the reference for following changes in the global coffee market.

After the collapse of ICA, prices dropped dramatically and stayed low for five years. Countries dependent on coffee exports suffered drastic drops in their export earnings within a few months, and worldwide earnings from coffee dropped $5 billion (Dicum and Luttinger 1999). In 1994 frosts in Brazil caused world prices to double, but they fell again a few years later to reach the historically low coffee prices that prevailed until recently (see figure 3.2). Prices started rising again in 2004 and are expected to rise further as Hurricane Katrina may have affected the U.S. main coffee warehouses in New Orleans.

Reconfiguration of the Market

Due to the structural adjustment policies imposed by the World Bank and the International Monetary Fund in the 1980s and 1990s, most national coffee institutes, like INMECAFE in Mexico, by and large disappeared through budget cutting, and their infrastructure was privatized. These neoliberal reforms have had serious consequences for small farmers, particularly those in remote areas like the Lacandón jungle in Chiapas. These farmers traditionally depended on the national institutes for technical

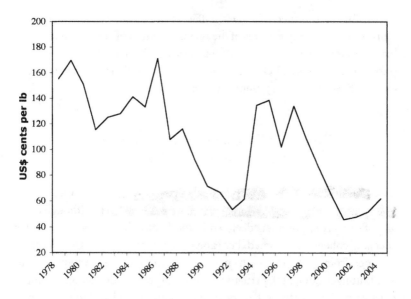

Figure 3.2. Average world coffee prices, 1976–2004.
Source: ICO composite indicator prices

assistance, credit, subsidized transport to market centers, and processing. Taken together, the changes in the international (breaking up of ICA) and national (privatization of coffee institutes) regulatory frameworks for coffee, changes in technology, and changes in the structure of demand constitute a major reconfiguration of the global coffee commodity system since the 1980s.

A key feature of the system that developed after the 1989 breakup of the International Coffee Agreement was the broadening of quality-based pricing originally based on four categories: Colombian milds, other milds (both washed arabicas), arabicas (not washed), and robustas. These categories are based on flavor, which depends in turn on the species of coffee tree (*arabica* or *robusta*) the beans come from, the method of harvesting, whether only ripe berries are picked, and the processing method (wet or dry). Today there are an infinite number of definitions of quality, like the denomination of origin (e.g., Guatemala Altiplano, or Pluma Hidalgo), which significantly add to the quality component of value added. This has opened a plethora of new opportunities to access specialty coffee markets for small-scale producers (organic coffee, shade-grown coffee, and so on). This is one of the key features of the reconfiguration of coffee demand that has impacted small farmers in Mesoamerica, as dozens of new alternative trade organizations (ATOs) have sprung up to help them market their specialty coffees (Meda 1995; Simpson and Rapone 1998).

Changes in Consumption: The Emergence of New Specialty Coffee Markets

The rapidly growing demand for so-called *specialty* (*gourmet* and *organic*) coffee is a result of recent changes in consumption patterns. Although overall coffee consumption has declined in the United States, the demand for specialty coffees has boomed. Per capita consumption in the United States dropped from thirty-six gallons per year in 1970 to twenty in 1996 (Dicum and Luttinger 1999, 142), perhaps as a result of competition among younger consumers by substitute beverages like sodas, and also due to growing health concerns about caffeine (Junguito and Pizano 1993; see figure 3.3). Thanks to the historic dominance of large roasters in the United States, most coffee sold was preground and packaged in vacuum-packed bricks or cans, with little regard to quality (appearance or aroma). The last few years have been marked by the appearance of the very dynamic specialty coffee market segment, which in 2003 expanded to 35 percent of the U.S. coffee industry (SCAA 2003). The rise of the "third space"—neither home nor office—like gourmet cafés highly frequented, has played a key role in driving changing patterns of consumption. Nevertheless, the United States is still the single largest coffee-importing market in the world, with imports of over 1.13 billion kilos in 2004 (USDA 2005).

In Europe, organic coffee was the first specialty coffee. Decades before the reconfiguration of the market, *Café de Altura,* organic coffee grown on the pioneering organic *Finca Irlanda* in the Soconusco region of Chiapas, had carved out a niche in health-food stores in Germany. Organic coffee is by far the most successful specialty coffee. This market grew 20 percent during the 1990s in northern countries as a whole (Thrupp 1997), and by 23 percent in the United States. This growing demand represents an enormous opportunity that small farmers who produce high-quality organic coffee are now taking advantage of.

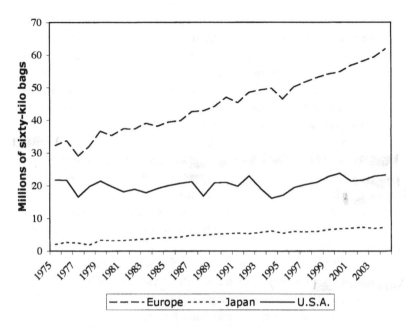

Figure 3.3. Coffee consumption by ICO members, 1975–2004.
Source: ICO members' historical data, 2005

Alternative Trade and Fair Trade

The concept of alternative trade was born in Europe as a way to address the inequity of international trade in which the former colonial powers set prices and producers in the former colonies have no choice but to accept them. During the 1960s a political movement evolved to counter the organization of production and trade around abstract market principles that devalue and exploit disadvantaged peoples and the environment, particularly in poorer regions of the south (Raynolds 2000, 2). Out of this fair trade movement came the establishment, throughout western Europe, of a chain of more than three hundred small solidarity shops, which sell "socially responsible" products. The shops are either privately owned or run by local voluntary committees or nongovernmental organizations (NGOs) (Nigh 1992). Mexican organic coffee cooperatives like Unión de Comunidades Indígenas de la Región del Istmo (UCIRI) and Indígenas de la Sierra Madre de Motozintla "San Isidro Labrador" (ISMAM) market their products in these stores.

This movement created an alternative market chain that goes from the coffee producer co-op to the European sister alternative trade organization and their shops and another three hundred informal distribution points. Greenfield (1994) reported that ATOs have focused on coffee as their lever of change, and that this is the export crop in which alternative trade can make the most difference.[2] More organizations have since joined this movement, where ATOs are linked to notions of alternative or "sustainable" rural development (Luttinger and Dicum 1999). They seek to transform the conditions that maintain poverty in rural areas by providing poor peasants with new marketing channels, technical assistance, and new products, like organic coffee, that may bring them higher prices (Greenfield 1994; Meda 1995; Nigh 1992). These organizations often run small rural programs in which farmers are trained in alternative production and marketing techniques.

In the United States, this solidarity market was pioneered in 1985 by Equal Exchange, the first ATO to sell coffee, in support of Nicaragua and in defiance of the U.S. trade embargo against that country. This worker-owned commercial cooperative continues buying coffee today under fair trade (see below) conditions, from small farmers all over the world. Although coffee constitutes more than half the volume of all alternative trade (Renard 1999, 182), this mechanism actually handles a very small percentage of the total coffee market, and therefore benefits only a small number of producers.

In 1986 at a meeting in Oaxaca, UCIRI told Solidaridad, a Dutch ecumenical NGO, that they would not need grants if coffee prices would cover their production costs and allow their families a decent standard of living (Max Havelaar 1995, cited in Wohlgemuth 1996). This prompted a process of consultations, negotiations, and meetings that came up with what we know today as the fair trade label. The idea was to create a label that would require certain standards and conditions and that regular market players (importers, distributors, roasters) could plug into their already established brands. The conditions included direct purchasing from small farmer cooperatives and a fixed price that would offer better living conditions to the farm families. This step led in turn to the need for a certifying organization that would not only protect the authenticity of the process and the label but would take into account the best interests of both producers and consumers. It was with this mission that Max Havelaar, a foundation of religious groups, alternative trade groups, development agencies, consumers, roasters, and representatives from the producers' co-ops, was created in the Netherlands in 1988 (Renard 1999).

The name Max Havelaar was chosen after the name of the book that denounced the terrible conditions that the Indonesian population was subjected to by the Dutch East Indies Company (190). Unlike the alternative-trade market, this initiative attempted to enter the regular market, counting on the existence of consumers who were willing to stand behind their beliefs. The founders hoped that by proving the existence of this market segment, they might have a positive influence on other participants in the coffee market chain (191). Max Havelaar registers coffee producer organizations, sets the buying conditions, grants roasters licences to use the label, maintains controls on both producers and roasters, and promotes the initiative among consumers to boost demand. To finance the initiative, the holders of a license pay royalties for the use of the label on each kilo they sell. The holders of licenses can put the label on packages of coffee bought directly from registered producer co-ops. Originally the minimum price to farmers was US$1.65 per pound, or a 10 percent premium over the world market price if that should ever rise above $1.65. The buyers are committed to prepaying up to 60 percent of the contract, and thus help finance the harvest. The success of the initiative in the Netherlands was followed by other European groups, who set up Max Havelaar foundations in their own countries. During the early 1990s, Belgium, Switzerland, Germany, Great Britain, France, Denmark, Austria, and Luxemburg opened fair trade foundations, with coordinated but autonomous functions (206).

At the same time, the alternative trade organizations decided to expand their operations, and formed the European Fair Trade Association (EFTA[3]) in 1990 (EFTA 1998). They created the TransFair label, which is similar to Max Havelaar, but with central coordination from their office in Germany. They guaranteed a minimum price for producers of US$1.10 per pound, later raised to US$1.26, a price that took into account the cost of production. When selling under fair trade conditions, farmers cannot receive less than this floor price. In 1997, TransFair opened an office in the United States where Fair Trade Certified coffee has become the fastest-growing segment of the U.S. specialty coffee market (TransFair 2005). The movement for organic and fair trade coffee is such that in 1999, the city of Berkeley, California, declared that municipal offices would buy only organic coffee, and only with the fair trade label (Selna 1999).

After the other U.S. fair trade organizations joined EFTA, they formed the Fair Trade Labeling Organizations International, in 1997 (Raynolds 2000; Rice and McLean 1999). They have agreed on a common table of prices (see table 3.2) for all fair trade initiatives, with a premium of US five cents over the international coffee price if this goes above the minimum. Organic coffee also gets a fifteen-cent premium. According to Rice and McLean, fair trade benefits three hundred cooperatives from Latin America, Asia, and Africa, with a total membership of 550,000 small-scale coffee farmers. In 1998, 25 million pounds of fair trade coffee were sold in Europe, with a retail value of US$200 million.

THE RISE OF THE LABELING GAME

The differentiation of the global coffee market into specialty coffee categories and the rise of fair trade labels have generated a profusion of competing label initiatives over the last few years. Labels give information to consumers about the conditions—environmental or social or both—under

TABLE 3.2
Minimum fair trade coffee prices in US cents per pound

	Nonorganic Central America, Mexico, Africa	South America, Caribbean
Arabica washed	126	124
Arabica non-washed	120	120
Robusta washed	110	110
Robusta non-washed	106	106
	Organic Central America, Mexico, Africa	South America, Caribbean
Arabica washed	141	139
Arabica non-washed	135	135
Robusta washed	125	125
Robusta non-washed	121	121

Source: Renard 1999, 223

which the coffee was produced. Many coffee labeling terms have emerged as part of the increasingly specialized coffee market. *Organic,* the first such term, is the most recognizable, but *fair trade, conservation coffee, bird-friendly, shade-grown,* and *sustainable coffee* all compete for a share of the specialty market. Many of these categories are connected with of the criteria for certification that its producers have to meet.

Within any given category—"shade coffee," for example—the criteria vary among the brands vying for certification. In an important comparative study, Alexandre Mas and Thomas Dietsch (2000) field-tested some of these shade coffee labels from five different coffee farms in Chiapas and found a wide variation in certification criteria (see table 3.3).

A consumer interest study by the Canadian Commission for Environmental Cooperation (CEC 1999) found that one-fifth of the coffee consumers in Canada, Mexico City, and the United States were very interested in purchasing Mexican shade-grown coffee, primarily because it provides better habitat for migratory birds and other wildlife.[4] However, U.S. consumers were less willing than Canadians and Mexicans to pay an extra dollar per pound for shade-grown coffee. The results also showed that flavor was a more important key factor in consumer choice, surpassing concern for environmental issues in all three countries.

There are also many labels already on the market that are not certified, since regional differences in natural vegetations and microclimate make it hard to standardized shade certification requirements. Rice and McLean (1999) estimate $15 million in sales in 1998 of shade-grown coffee, most of it uncertified and mainly from Mexico and Central America.

The most recent label initiative is *sustainable coffee.* Since the 1996 Sustainable Coffee Congress organized by the Smithsonian Institution in Washington, DC, the concept of sustainable coffee has been subject to debate. It was a move by the Smithsonian itself, in an attempt to put together all the new labels that were suddenly on the market and ensure that real ecological criteria were included. In the Second Sustainable Coffee Congress held in Denver in 1998, the discussions about a definition continued, this time recognizing that the term *sustainability* has different meanings for different agroecological regions and organizations. Sustainable coffee means coffee that is produced with few chemical inputs, in a system that conserves biodiversity. The idea is that it is environmentally sound and commercially competitive, and improves the quality of life of

TABLE 3.3
Results of applications for shade certification criteria, Chiapas

Certification Program	Belen Traditional Rustic	Belen Production	Irlanda Buffer Zone	Irlanda Production	Hamburgo Production
	Farm that applied for certification				
	Number of certification criteria met by the farm/result of certification				
SCAA, Specialty Coffee Association/3 criteria	3, Shade	3, Shade	3, Shade	3, Shade	2, Not Shade
EKO Ok, Rain Forest Alliance/8 criteria	8, Certify	7, Borderline	8, Certify	8, Certify	5, Reject
Bird Friendly, Smithsonian Institute/7 Criteria	7, Certify	3, Reject	6, Borderline	5, Reject	3, Reject
Mexican Shade/7 criteria	7, Certify	4, Reject	6, Borderline	4, Reject	2, Reject
Mexican Shade Plus/7 criteria	7, Certify	1, Reject	4, Reject	4, Reject	2, Reject
Total certifications	5	2	2	2	0

Source: Mas and Dietsch 2000

farmers and society (Greenberg 2001). Nevertheless, from a marketing point of view, sustainability is a difficult idea to sell to U.S. consumers.

In 2002, eleven Mexican organizations of coffee producers, seven nonprofits, three certification programs, and a few academics formed the Consejo Civil para la Cafeticultura Sustentable en Mexico (CCCSM, Mexican Sustainable Coffee Civic Council). Their aim is to promote and consolidate the concept of sustainable coffee in Mexico, including high coffee quality, organic production under diversified shade, and fair trade certification. In contrast with other "sustainable" coffees that only certify shade, this Mexican concept integrates the social, economical and environmental dimensions of sustainability.

THE MARKET FOR all specialty coffees has been very dynamic in the last few years. By 2003, retail sales of these high-quality coffees in the United States alone passed US$1.7 billion of the $5 billion U.S. coffee industry, and this sector continues to grow rapidly (SCAA 2003). At this point all major coffee players have launched their own specialty coffee brands, like Philip Morris's Gevalia mail-order business, with $100 million in revenues (Dicum and Luttinger 1999, 150). In tune with the demand for specialty coffee, demand for instant coffee has dropped, but the overall consumption of roasted coffee is up. Japan recently entered the coffee market as a consumer, and its demand is exploding. In Europe demand for specialty coffee is also rising. There was a small boom in decaffeinated coffee in the United States in the 1980s, but it tapered off in the 1990s, largely due to health concerns about the chemicals used[5] to extract the caffeine (Junguito and Pizano 1993).

Large corporations have also launched their own efforts to compete with the social criteria labels, like Max Havelaar or TransFair, by marketing their coffee as produced by small-scale growers. Examples of this include the Douwe Egberts (Sara Lee) media campaign in Belgium to promote *Boerenkoffie* (peasant coffee), and the independent German roaster Jacobs launch of its new brand Café Cóndor, from coffee co-ops in Peru (Renard 1999, 224). When Starbucks started selling a tiny proportion of its coffee under the fair trade label, a controversial discussion ensued on "how fair is fair trade," given the widespread perception that Starbucks uses unethical practices to drive independent "mom and pop" coffee shops out of business around the world.

There is also a growing literature analyzing and criticizing the imagery used in the marketing of so-called alternative consumption products, which includes coffee produced by poor farmers (Goodman 2004; Jaffee, Kloppenburg, and Monroy 2004). The criticism centers around the tendency to market fair trade commodities using colonial-style imagery of "noble savages," while reinforcing international flows that have remained essentially unchanged since colonialism. Rather than promoting local trade in domestic markets, which would arguably contribute more to local and national economic development, most fair trade still promotes export product, albeit with somewhat better prices (Raymond and Goodman 2004, 345). A similar criticism exists for organic products: despite the fact that urban consumers may develop an environmental consciousness through buying organic food products, the responsibility for taking care of the environment, or the blame for not doing so, continues to lie squarely on poor people in rural areas, thus allowing urban consumers to assuage their conscience without addressing the environmental impacts of urban lifestyles (González, Linck, and Moguel 2003). However, for Mexican small-scale growers' organizations the biggest challenge is to grapple effectively with the tyranny of world coffee markets through the ever-changing prices.

Changes in Prices

Green coffee is sold in a variety of international markets, which include the spot market, the shipment market, the futures markets, and the cash trade. The spot market trades in coffee that has arrived from producing countries and is already in warehouses. These negotiations take place among importers, brokers, and roasters. In the shipment market, coffee that is available for shipment is sold before it has left the producing country. The establishment in 1882 of the only U.S. futures market in New York, as a way of protecting buying companies against price fluctuations, implied a power shift in the coffee commodity chain from commercial capital to financial capital (Arenas 1981). In a futures market, prices are determined by a market assessment of what the price will be at a future date of purchase. Futures markets are often thought of as a mechanism for traders to hedge against price fluctuations, and conversely, as a way for investors to gamble on price fluctuations by speculating. The hedger expects to need to buy or sell at a future date, and, rather than risk less favorable prices in the future, buys or sells contracts for future delivery. The speculator assumes the risks of price fluctuation in order to make profits, by predicting the direction in which the market will move; these speculative transactions account for 15 percent of coffee trades (Rice and McLean 1999).

Export coffee prices are fixed in relation to the volatile New York Board of Trade futures contract for washed arabica beans, the so-called C contract. Coffee from each country or region receives a premium or discount known as differential against the C, depending on quality. Colombian *excelso* has a positive differential of ten to fourteen points over the base price, while Mexican coffee has a five-to-ten-point discount, due to its past variability in quality. This negative differential was as high as twenty-five points in the 1998–99 harvest, reflecting the power of transnational buyers to fix prices.

The volatility of the NYCE C contract is mostly due to speculation, usually by large mutual funds, and to major weather events (like a freeze in Brazil). During the 1990s the price was generally very low, although it swung from US$0.48 per pound (extremely low) to US$2.71 per pound (very high). The price paid to farmers is pegged to the C contract price, though the fraction of the total selling price that they receive also depends on the chain of intermediaries involved in the transaction. An approximate calculation is that when the C price is eighty-five cents per pound, the farmer might receive twenty to forty cents per pound (see figure 3.4). Organic coffee buyers always pay a price above the base price. Organic price premiums—currently between five and twenty cents per pound—are fixed by agreements among the buyers and their clients and less by supply and demand (AICA 1997).

The average worldwide coffee price is reflected in the International Coffee Organization composite price. The procedures for collecting, transmitting, calculating and publishing the ICO composite price are agreed upon among signatories of the current ICA. Since October 2003, the calculation of the composite price has been based on a complex formula. To calculate the ICO composite price, the four categories themselves then are weighted in determining the overall composite price (see table 3.4). For comparative historical price data, the weighting is 13 percent of Colombian milds, 27 percent of other milds, 25 percent of Brazilian naturals, and 35 percent of robustas.

43

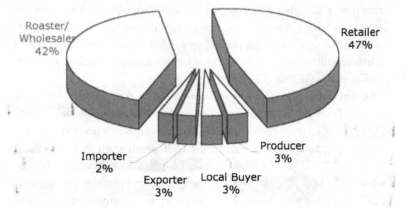

Figure 3.4. Distribution of coffee price, 1999. *Note:* Percentages based on "C" contract price (US$0.85/lb). *Source:* Rice and McLean 1999, 21

TABLE 3.4
Weightings in coffee composite price

Weighting of markets shares per category	Weighting of New York & German prices
Colombian Milds	40% New York-60% Germany
Other Milds	50% New York-50% Germany
Brazilian Naturals	20% New York-80% Germany
Robustas	20% New York-80% France

Source: ICO 2003

However, the prices received by producers at the farm gate or co-op fluctuate daily, or even several times during the same day, and not just in accordance with the New York Coffee Exchange (NYCE) and the quality differential, but also depending on the variable availability of accurate international pricing information. These variables makes price a tricky and sensitive issue. A farmer can sell at one price in the morning while in the afternoon a buyer might pay a higher price to a neighboring farmer. Furthermore, during the harvest season the same farmer will, in all probability, sell the beans collected during the different harvest passes at different prices (see figure 3.5). The complicated and variable nature of coffee

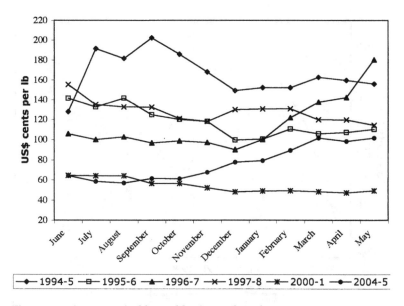

Figure 3.5. Average monthly world prices, selected years.
Source: ICO monthly members' statistical data, 2005

pricing, complicated by the lack of accurate information for local actors, is very difficult for an ordinary person to grasp, all too often forcing small farmers to guess or gamble whether to sell right away or wait for a better price.

As one can see in figure 3.6, the actual price received by coffee growers varies from country to country, and also changes over time. This is the result of a series of factors and their interactions, including international price flucuations, quality-based pricing, and the relationships between intermediaries (public and private) and farmers.

Expanding the Mexican Coffee Market

Although specializing in coffee makes cooperatives of small-scale coffee producers dependent on the international market, these organizations have recognized this weakness and have been leading the way toward expansion of the consumption of quality coffee inside Mexico. The country's

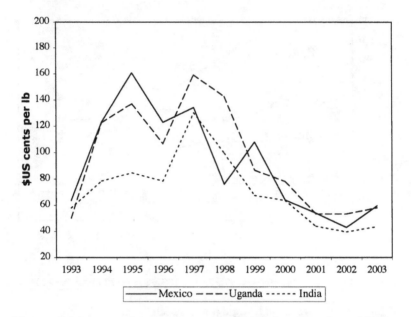

Figure 3.6. Average prices paid to growers in Mexico, Uganda, and India, 1993–2003. *Source:* ICO members' statistical data, 2004

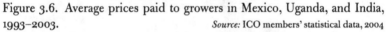

total coffee consumption has long been very low compared to that of top coffee-consuming countries, but that is beginning to change as small cafés and coffee shops have sprung up all over Mexican cities and towns during the past ten to fifteen years. This began when cooperatives of small-scale coffee growers opened their own coffee shops to showcase their wares to the Mexican consuming public, and they were soon followed by numerous other cafés owned by independent entrepreneurs, and consumption patterns have begun to shift. The opening of coffee shops by coffee cooperatives is a development strategy targeting the local and national markets. This strategy has been used successfully by other farmer groups in Latin America—as in the case of wine in Argentina (Posada and Velarde 2000). When such strategies meet with success, they make the producer less dependent on the vagaries of the international market. At the same time, producer organizations are strengthened, and they may capture more of the value added from their product, as in the case of coffee, where the organization also handles the roasting, packaging, and retailing. The

Mexican Coffee Council estimates Mexico's internal coffee market to have consumed 1 million bags in 1995, with Nestlé dominating the instant coffee market (cited in CEC 1999).

These initiatives are exemplified by coffee cooperatives like Coordinadora Estatal de Productores de Café de Oaxaca (CEPCO), and the Unión de Ejidos de la Selva (La Selva) in Chiapas. La Selva now has four cafés in Mexico City and one café each in San Cristóbal de las Casas (Chiapas), Guadalajara, and Monterrey. They have even started opening franchises abroad, and had the first overseas café, in Barcelona, Spain. La Selva is now negotiating to open a franchise in Atlanta, Georgia. The owners of the franchises commit to buy all their coffee from La Selva farmers.

A similar example is the Café Museo in San Cristóbal de las Casas, where coffee from small farmer associations is sold. This space has become a center for cultural events and a meeting place for activists, NGOs, and researchers. Café Museo also set up a remarkable permanent exposition on the coffee production process and on the lives of coffee-growing families. Today many coffee co-ops in Mexico are opening local shops and cafés, though the recent entry of Starbucks into the Mexican market may put all of them in danger. Nevertheless, for Mexican peasant producer organizations, the biggest challenge is still how to navigate the changing terrain of the world coffee market.

The recent reconfigurations of the coffee market globally, and in Mexico, set the stage for the developments among the organizations of small-scale coffee farmers in Chiapas. A key feature of this reconfiguration was the collapse of the International Coffee Agreement (ICA) and subsequent market segmentation with the emergence of new niche markets for gourmet coffee, organic coffee, fair trade coffee, and other specialty products, some of which have opened entry points for organizations of small farmers.

Overall, the emergence of new technologies and the reconfiguring of markets have both generated problems and created opportunities for organizations of coffee farmers. In Mexico, the rise of neoliberal economic policies, and in particular the privatization of the Mexican Coffee Institute, further reshaped the conditions faced by small farmers. The following two chapters examine how small-scale coffee producers in Chiapas created organizations capable of confronting those challenges.

Chapter 4

The Geography and History of Coffee in Chiapas

As in the rest of Mesoamerica, coffee growing across the varied history and geography of Mexico and Chiapas is characterized by a high degree of social and economic heterogeneity. There is and has been a great diversity of production systems that include both large plantations and tiny groves, both free and forced labor, both exorbitant accumulation of wealth in the hands of a few and a broader distribution income. In some places, the power and wealth derived from this sector of the economy are concentrated in the hands of the older oligarchy (Guatemala and El Salvador); in others coffee helped consolidate new agro-export elites (El Salvador); in still others an important peasant coffee sector developed (Nicaragua), and in a few countries a broad sector of small-scale coffee producers became the economic basis of a rural middle class based on family labor and occasional paid labor (Honduras and Costa Rica) (Pérez and Samper 1994, 10–11). All these social arrangements can be found in the history of coffee production in Mexico and Chiapas.

The coffee-growing areas of Chiapas are located on the mountain ranges running northwest to southeast, parallel to the coast (see map 4.1). They are part of the belt of young mountains that extends along the west coast of the Americas, which are essentially folds in the underlying tectonic plates created by the enormous pressure from the slow collision between the American continental plate and the Pacific Ocean plate. The

48

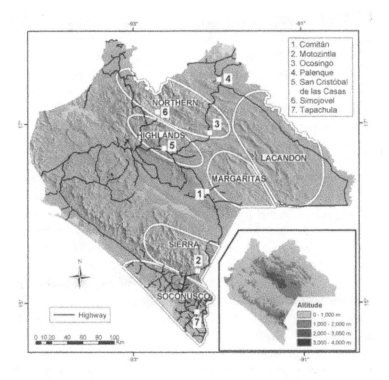

Map 4.1. Coffee-producing regions of Chiapas

prime areas for coffee production in Chiapas—the Soconusco, Los Altos (highlands), the sierra, the north, and the jungle—demonstrate a rich diversity of microclimates and biological habitats.

The Soconusco and Sierra Regions

The Soconusco region encompasses a coastal plain and a mountain range with altitudes up to four thousand meters above sea level. The climate is tropical, with 2,500 to 5,000 mm of rainfall annually, and there are a number of rivers and evergreen forests in the mountains. The Soconusco has the best soils for coffee production and produces 65 percent of the coffee in Chiapas. In large part because of its historic role as a major coffee export center, the region has port facilities, a railroad, and a major city and commercial center: Tapachula, near the border with Guatemala.

The sierra region is located in the Sierra Madre of Chiapas, a skeletal frame of metamorphic Paleozoic rocks with granite intrusions that is oriented east to west (Pohlenz 1995). Ranging from one to three thousand meters above sea level, this fractured terrain has a dryer climate than other parts of Chiapas. The main commercial center of the sierra is the town of Motozintla, also near the Guatemalan border.

The Soconusco (from *Xoconoshco,* the place of the *xoconoshtli,* Nahuatl for a bitter cactus fruit) was the first region in Chiapas to produce coffee. Coffee was introduced there in 1846 by an Italian entrepreneur on the La Chacara finca.[1] Before the arrival of the Spanish, Xoconoshco was the principal source of cocoa seeds in the Aztec empire, which they used as currency, and for the highly prized quetzal feathers used by the nobility. It was sparsely inhabited, mainly by various Central American indigenous groups (Mangues, Pipiles,[2] and Nicaraos), coexisting with the neighboring Mayan Mams from Tacana, the sierra Tuzantecos[3] and Tectitecos, and the coastal Tapachultecos (Schumann 1969). Over time, as the population grew, these groups mixed and created a new culture.

During the eighteenth and first half of the nineteenth centuries the Spanish fincas in Chiapas produced cacao, which they exported to Guatemala and the rest of Mexico. A decline in coffee production in the main Guatemalan producing region of Costa de Cuca and higher coffee prices (due to a revolution in Brazil), led to the promotion of coffee production in the Soconusco. Given favorable ecological conditions and the low cost of land, coffee production in the Soconusco took off.[4]

In 1883 the liberal Ley de Colonización decreed the division of public lands into parcels, which allowed survey companies[5] to sell large extensions of land to individual landholders (Renard 1993; Calva 1993). This law was a product of the need of the Mexican state to colonize its border with Guatemala, in response to the Guatemalan government's territorial claims over the Soconusco.[6] This law was key in the expansion of coffee fincas in the Soconusco and the sierra. Many colonists came from other parts of Mexico, as well as from countries like England, the United States, and France. They were small farmers who combined the cultivation of sugar cane and refining of sugar to sustain themselves between good coffee harvests (Renard 1993). German coffee producers also came, from Guatemala, and brought technical knowledge and experience with producing coffee with them, as well as machinery and professional administrators (Helbig 1964; Renard 1993). By 1908 there were sixty-six coffee farms in Chiapas (Weibel 1933, cited in Renard 1993).

The significant and specialized labor needs for coffee cultivation greatly determined the pace of development of the new coffee plantations. The establishment of a coffee grove is very labor intensive during the first five years. According to Williams (1994), approximately 15 percent of the labor costs of setting up a big plantation is typically spent germinating seeds and caring for seedlings in the nursery, while 40 percent is spent preparing the fields and planting, and in the first year of crop care and maintenance. Because of the mountainous terrain in which coffee is grown, trucks and tractors cannot bring seedlings to plant—humans must carry the seedlings onto the slopes. The work is arduous and risky. In the Soconusco and the sierra, finca owners could not find enough workers to meet these heavy labor needs. To solve the labor shortage, owners started the practice of *enganche* (hooking) at the beginning of the 1900s, in which they sent a labor recruiter to contract (*enganchar*) workers in the highlands. They offered potential workers good salaries, advanced their pay, and then brought them as a group to the finca by foot or other transportation; all costs for food and other basic needs were also advanced by the owner (Renard 1993, 30). By the time they arrived at the finca, the worker had incurred an extensive debt from travel costs that he had to work to pay off. Through this system of indentured servitude, the owners could count on a stable work force all year long. In addition, campesinos from Guatemala would come to work for the harvest season (Helbig 1964; Renard 1993; field notes).

Over time the finca system spread across all regions of Chiapas. The nature of the servitude imposed on the workers eventually led to indigenous rebellions in the highlands and northern regions (Moscoso 1992) and to the organization of farmworker unions in the Soconusco. Virtually all the indentured laborers on the Soconusco fincas joined unions, and almost all these eventually became so-called agrarian committees (Pohlenz 1995).[7] Many of these committees then received land through the agrarian reform in the middle of the twentieth century.

Era una finca, el dueño se llamaba Antonio Baleras y pues este, se pusieron los trabajadores, ahora si que a pelear de acuerdo en el tiempo de don Lázaro Cárdenas y este si, vino la orden y órale a descuartizar la finca y se logro de esa manera y muchos no lo creían, y pero si fue cierto. Hoy todavía hay al-gunas fincas por hay perdidas que dicen ya no le dio tiempo repartirlas.

There was a finca, the owner was named Antonio Baleras, and with him, yes, the workers united and started fighting in the time of Mr. Lázaro Cár-denas [president of Mexico in the 1930s, who initiated the first major agrarian reform], and he, yes, he gave the order, oh yeah, to chop up the finca this way. That's how we got it, though many at that time didn't be-lieve it was true, but it was. Though I guess there are still a few fincas here and there that he didn't have time to redistribute.

José Morales, mestizo coffee farmer from Unión Juárez, Soconusco.

The Soconusco became the first and most important agrarian capitalist region of Chiapas with the production, processing, and commercialization of coffee (Pohlenz 1995). This is the only region where modern "high" technology production methods were implemented in coffee during the 1980s (for a description of the different technologies, see chapter 2). Al-though the Soconusco is the most industrialized coffee area, only 4.6 per-cent of producers are large private farms: the rest are small producers (Villafuerte and Meza 1993).

Los Altos and the Northern Region

The highlands (Los Altos) are oriented from northwest to southeast, with altitudes ranging from twelve to sixteen hundred meters above sea level. The western highlands are displaced faults, while the eastern highlands are mainly folds of sedimentary formations—mainly limestone, shale, and sandstone (Mera 1989). The highlands climate in the Koeppen modified classification system for Mexico (E. Garcia 1982) is humid temperate C(m) and subhumid temperate $C(w_2)(w)$. This climate exhibits a summer rainy season and a dry winter, with possibilities of frost from December to March. The region is characterized by thin, rocky cam-bisol, andosol, litosol, and rendzinas soils (FAO-UNESCO classifica-tion) (Mera 1989).

With the publication of the Ley de Obreros in 1914, serfs liberated from the fincas in the Soconusco returned to their indigenous towns in the highlands, bringing the agronomic practices of the finca with them. The mostly Tzeltal and Tzotzil indigenous people who worked on the coffee plantations took actual seedlings with them and planted them in their newly granted land, while those who worked on cattle ranches established small-scale cattle ranching on their new land (Craipeau 1993; Marquez 1990). There was a great deal of resistance at first to adopting coffee in the highlands, because there was still no market for it there and because of the large amount of time required to establish a coffee grove. It was not until there were middlemen to buy their coffee that campesinos began to seriously produce it, and many then stopped migrating for seasonal work to obtain cash for their needs.

Antes pues me dijo mi papa, no quieren sembrar café porque cuando se cosecha no puede vender y nadie quien comprar, por eso no quieren sembrar mas matas pues lo siembra un poquito pero para tomar nomás. Cuando ellos lo vieron que hay compradores de café, ahí lo empezaron de sembrar café pues. De ahí encontramos dinero para comprar algo de ropa. Ahorita ni sale en otro lugar para conseguir dinero, ya no, aquí nomás produce su café cuando es tiempo cosecha.

My papa told me that before, nobody wanted to plant coffee since once you harvested it you couldn't sell, since nobody wanted to buy it. That's why they didn't want to transplant more coffee plants, they just put in a few for coffee to drink, and no more. But when they saw the coffee buyers begin to arrive, that's when they started to really plant. That's when we started to have enough money to buy some clothes. Now we don't go elsewhere to earn money, we just sell coffee at harvest time.

Abelardo Rodriguez, Tzotzil coffee producer, Poconichim, Eastern Highlands.

In the highlands in the 1960s the National Indigenous Institute (INI) became the main agency promoting the adoption of coffee as a possible way out of extreme poverty. But it was only after the peasant land invasions of coffee farms in the highlands and northern regions in 1974 that coffee truly became a widespread part of the production of most individual farms (Parra and Moguel 1996).

Empezamos a sembrar café cuando empezamos a solicitar y vino este programa del INI y nos dio prestado ese trabajo, ahora cada quien su parcela, a sembrar café, cada quien a su parcela a limpiar, ya cuando empezó a dar fruta entonces ahí si empezamos a comprar máquina [despulpadora] por grupo de socios de diez en diez. Porque no había muchos cafetales, lo hicimos en grupo, ahora ya cuando avanzó el café cada quien tiene su máquina.

We began to plant coffee when we started to ask for land, and then this program came from the INI and they showed us this work. Now each one had their own plot to plant coffee, each one weeded their plot, and when the harvests started coming in, then we started buying machines [depulpers] in groups of ten partners. At that time nobody had that much coffee, so we bought the machines in groups, but today, with the increase in production, everyone has their own machine.

Raymundo González, tzotzil producer from San Miguel, Western Highlands.

Some municipalities in the Highlands did not produce coffee before 1970, yet by 1990 there was a 900 percent increase in the total area planted (see table 4.1). Since the quality of the coffee beans depends partly on the elevation in which the crop is grown (Rice 1997, 130), the highlands are ideal for cultivating high-quality coffee. Today the coffee-producing area of the highlands includes the municipalities of Oxchuc, Panteló, El Bosque, Tenejapa, Chenalhó, San Andrés Larráinzar, and Chalchihuitán, with some six thousand producers in 107 communities. In this region, formal organizations of small coffee producers were the product of the support from the INI and the Mexican Coffee Institute (INMECAFE) (Parra and Moguel 1996, 23).

TABLE 4.1
Area planted with coffee in Los Altos, 1970–90

Municipality	Planted coffee in hectares	
	1970	1990
Chalchihuitan	31	1,917
Chenalho	41	2,691
Larrainzar	1	605
Oxchuc	0	1,581
Pantelho	1,276	2,553
Tenejapa	2	3,132
Teopisca	37	310
Total	1,388	12,789

Source: Martínez Quezada 1990. Data from Censo Agrícola Ganadero y Ejidal, 1970, 1990

Among the many kinds of formal organizations in Chiapas (and there were over two thousand organizations there in 1995, according to a survey by ECOSUR), the organizations of small coffee producers have the most members and are very active. Of 152 organizations in the highlands (less than 10 percent of the total in Chiapas), only nineteen are coffee producer organizations. Yet these producer organizations, with over twelve thousand registered members, account for just over two-thirds of the total membership in formal organizations in Chiapas (Parra and Moguel 1995). By 1990 just two organizations (Majomut and COTZEPEC) accounted for 30 percent of the coffee producers in the highlands (Martínez Quezada 1990). In 1993 and 1994 there were mobilizations in Panthelhó, Cancuc, Larráinzar, and Chalchihuitán to channel government resources through the INI and the Pronasol social program. The main demand was to get financial support for coffee cultivation (just like Pronasol offered for corn production), and in 1995 growers in this region obtained seven hundred pesos per hectare.

TO THE NORTH of the highlands lies a region of geologic folds with lower altitudes, between seven and twelve hundred meters above sea level, and a tropical subhumid climate. Mixed forest and jungle are the main vegetation types. In contrast to the Soconusco, in this northern region the fincas traditionally relied on land evictions and the application of other coercive measures to access the locally abundant labor supply (Muench 1982, cited in Wohlgemuth 1996). Indigenous Tojolabal and Chol communities became sharecroppers or serfs on plantations and ranches and remained many generations, which made these ethnic groups more dependent on wealthy landowners than were other indigenous peoples in Chiapas (Köhler 2000, 201). In the region indigenous communities and the fincas merged their destinies so much that even the traditional indigenous *cargo* system[8] of community service and leadership was appropriated to support the system of servitude (Pérez 1989). Finally in the 1960s a redistribution of land ended forced labor in the northern region, which drove a shift in production patterns after which the fincas, deprived of their bound labor, became cattle ranches, while the campesino economy incorporated small amounts of coffee production to obtain cash (Cortés 1998; Martínez Quezada 1990; Pérez 1989).

Coffee Spreads to the Jungle

The jungle region, in eastern Chiapas, is formed by a series of canyonlike valleys, called the Cañadas, nestled between smaller mountain ridges oriented from northwest to southeast. Ranging from sea level to seven hundred meters, with some ridges reaching over a thousand meters, most of this region is covered by the Lacandón jungle. The soils of these jungle areas can sustain jungle vegetation, but once used for annual crop farming, the soils are good only for three or four harvests. A smaller jungle in the southern part of the region is the Margaritas jungle, with lower elevations (500–700 meters), from which the municipality of Margaritas takes its name.

From 1895 to 1913 the commercial logging of mahogany by Spanish, English, Belgian, and U.S. companies led to the extensive deforestation of the Lacandón region and to the construction of roads, which opened the way for colonization (Arizpe, Paz, and Velázquez 1998; Vos 1980). Around the turn of the century Porfirio Díaz gave the territory between the Chajul, Lacantún, Usumacinta, and Chixoy Rivers to the Márquez de Comillas, a Catalan entrepreneur, though a later government nationalized it in 1955 (Cortés 1998). Today that area is a buffer zone for the Montes Azules Biosphere Reserve, created in 1978 after national and international pressure to protect the jungle caused a shift in the governmental discourse toward conservation of natural resources (Harvey 1998).[9] Both the Márquez de Comillas and the nearby Cañadas zones were objects of colonization and contradictory governmental development projects (Cortés 1998; Harvey 1998).[10] The eastern part of this region was colonized by people from the highlands (mainly from Chamula, Huixtán, Tenejapa, and San Cristóbal de las Casas) in the 1960s, and testimonies from women show how they were forced by their husbands to move to the jungle (Garza et al. 1993).

> *Escucharon plática de que hay tierra libre y los hombres se fueron a pedir razón del terreno. Cuando lo encontraron vinieron a decir a sus esposas: vamonos para alla porque esta muy buena la tierra. Pero las mujeres no queriamos dejar los parajes. . . . no quiero abandonar a mi mama. . . . no quiero me da miedo el agua . . . ya estamos acostumbradas en Tierra Fria. Pero que vamos hacer si ya los hombres dijeron que nos vamos en Nacional. "Si no quieres venir, aquí te quedas," decía cada esposo y a algunas mujeres nos*

trajeron a la fuerza, con maltrato; en verdad solo unas pocas vinieron por su gusto.

They heard talk that there was empty land there, and the men went to seek vacant plots. When they found them they came to tell their wives, "Let's go there, because the land there is good." But we women didn't want to leave our parishes. . . . I didn't want to leave my mother. . . . I was afraid of the water we would have to cross . . . and we were used to living in the mountains. But what could we do if the men said let's go to the public lands? "If you don't want to come, then stay here [by yourself]," said each husband, and some of us women were dragged here by force, and they mistreated us; and the truth is only a few women came by their own free will.

testimony of a migrant woman (Garza et al. 1993, 35)

By the 1970s landless people, mainly from the highlands but also from all over Mexico, had populated the area (Collier 1996) and obtained land through the now-defunct agrarian reform program. The Montes Azules Biosphere Reserve was created by the forced relocation of people, with very meager development programs to compensate them. During the 1970s and 1980s there were some local community efforts to combine sustainable development programs with conservation, but the state government blocked them (Bray 1997). In the Cañadas zone,[11] Tzeltal, Tojolabal, mestizo, and Chol migrants developed an agricultural system based on corn and beans. They raised pigs, chickens, and turkeys to obtain cash and were aided in marketing the animals by the construction of dirt roads. Later they switched to coffee in the few places suitable to grow it, in some cases abandoning raising pigs because they damaged the coffee (Marquez 1990). The entire southern border became important in geopolitical terms in the 1980s due to several factors. Among these were the need to secure the border against the massive arrival of war refugees from Guatemala,[12] and the presence in the region of strategically important natural resources, such as petroleum and gas. During the 1990s, with NAFTA, the border with Guatemala also became the border of the North American economy with all of Central America (Embamex 1999).

Chapter 5

State, Society, and Rural Development in Mexico and Chiapas

THE GOVERNMENT OF Chiapas, despite some initially hopeful signs when the opposition was elected to the statehouse in 2001, has long been characterized as very conservative and repressive. While Chiapas had a major period of turmoil ending in 1863, in which more-conservative elites (based in the old capital city of San Cristóbal de las Casas) fought liberal ones (based in the current capital of Tuxtla Gutiérrez) to define state development policies, the landed oligarchy has been holding power since Mexican independence (García de Leon 1985). Basic citizen rights were long absent in most indigenous towns and rural areas until the 1960s. This situation changed during the last four decades, when the nature and intensity of relationships established between members of civil society—called *social capital*[1]—gave rise to strong peasant and indigenous organizations. The strength of civil society and its accumulated social capital is a key element in inducing effective government and generating economic development (Putnam 1993). Intense social mobilizations during the 1960s and 1970s opened political opportunities for social organizations across Mexico.

Social capital refers to those aspects of social structure that facilitate actions of individuals or groups who are part of the same social structure, namely social relations and norms (Coleman 1988). Social capital varies depending on group membership and social circumstance. Vertical networks that link certain state and civil society actors, which can have positive impacts on development, are an important part of social capital (North 1990). To understand the history of rural development in Mexico one must look at the interactions among central and local governments, national and local social organizations, leaders and representatives that mutually affect performance in development. The presence or absence of complementarities and partnerships within and across sectors that could develop synergies are key to understanding development processes (Evans 1996a, b; Ostrom 1996; Tendler 1995 and 1997).

The role of the state is both most important and most problematic. Only the state is big enough and has enough resources to bring about broad-based structural change, while communities can play a key role in creating conditions that reward good governance, and in difficult institutional situations, civil society leaders can identify and engage allies within an otherwise unfriendly state apparatus (Fox 1993). The extent to which the social capital of local organizations is "scaled up" through relationships between state, private, and voluntary organizations, to generate relationships of solidarity and social action on a larger and more important scale, can lead to different paths of development (Evans 1996b). In this sense, the history of coffee production is a good case through which to explain patterns of development and ultimately understand the push for more autonomous development by local organizations in Chiapas.

The 1960s and 1970s: Modernization and the Penetration of the State in Rural Areas

In response to the major social and political movements that swept Latin America in the 1960s, international financial institutions and governments adopted new development policies during the 1970s. The World Bank and USAID, among other donors, gave Latin American governments support for limited agrarian reform, access to credit for small farmers, and funding for research toward higher productivity in rural areas. In Mexico the state took on a regulatory role by partially protecting the peasant economy from market forces with price supports and tariffs against cheap imports. World Bank funds were channeled into Mexico's Rural Development Investment Program (PIDER) in response to campesino and social

59

mobilizations, and from 1976 to 1982 official policy supported productive projects throughout Mexico (Parra and Moguel 1996). The government implemented production-boosting programs including credit and subsidies for fertilizer and other inputs. In 1980 the Mexican Food System (SAM), a program designed to improve the distribution of food to the poor and reinvigorate peasant production through federal subsidies, was created. Many of these programs were designed to reverse a general anti-peasant bias in agricultural policy.

The governmental development programs required that campesinos be organized in bodies suitable for receiving credit in order to transfer funds. Laws were implemented to create various legal constructs for this purpose, such as the Unión de Ejidos (UE), the Unión de Uniones de Ejidos (UUE), the Asociación Rural de Interés Colectivo (ARIC), and the Asociación de Productores Rurales. The Mexican countryside was reorganized under these forms of association, opening spaces for participation even in places where there was no real freedom of association beyond the local village. It was during this period that campesinos learned to manage and organize their production collectively (beyond the family) and to deal with the market and the state. Some of the coffee farmer organizations formed in Chiapas during this time were the Unión de Uniones Ejidos de la Selva (La Selva), and the Unión de Crédito Pajal Yakaltik.

The rural development policies of the 1970s provided support for various sectors, such as coffee producers with the expansion of the Mexican Coffee Institute (INMECAFE) mandate in 1973, which began financing and processing coffee. For coffee farmers, INMECAFE became the alternative buyer to the middleman when its activities expanded to include not only technical assistance and research but also production credit, transport of harvests, processing, and marketing. Nevertheless, better-off peasants and larger farmers benefited disproportionately from these programs, in part due to a focus on increasing expenditures instead of restructuring institutions.

The state focused on the regulation of income—through such measures as minimum wages, subsidized food, and tax incentives—and of property ownership (e.g., foreigners could not own land) in order to balance the often contradictory challenges of economic growth and political stability, and "this model of regulation framed Mexico's political development until the economic crisis of 1982" (Fox 1994, 243). Nevertheless, this cycle of social capital formation, with its emphasis on financing for peasant production, left a number of new and relatively strong farmer organizations in Chiapas and elsewhere in rural Mexico.

The 1970s and 1980s: Indigenous Mobilization, Petroleum, and Debt Crisis

In 1974 the state government of Chiapas had felt the need for legitimation and requested that then bishop Samuel Ruiz organize a statewide Indigenous and Peasant Congress. The network of multilingual activists and lay Catholic catechists that bishop Ruiz had built up over the years was used to invite practically every community to participate. Although the government hoped to generate support for itself with this congress, the principal results were a new clarity of antigovernment sentiment in indigenous communities, and the creation of new relationships and networks of indigenous community representatives when they were able to meet and talk about their similar conditions and problems for the first time. The preparations for the congress, and the congress itself, catalyzed the growth of statewide organizations during the 1970s, especially those demanding land, and strengthened their connections to national organizations and national networks (Collier 1994; Odile and Singer 1983). This was the start of a long period of mobilization and organization throughout Chiapas that culminated twenty years later in the 1994 Zapatista uprising and continues to take shape today (Collier 1999; Wohlgemuth 1996).

Toward the end of the 1970s agriculture all over Mexico declined as Mexican oil prospered, an economic phenomenon caused by overvalued currency (the "Dutch Disease") that has been observed in many oil-producing countries. In Chiapas indigenous peasants were drawn into wage work and away from farming—their traditional source of income—by the energy development boom in the neighboring state of Tabasco (Collier 1994, 1999). In the rest of Mexico, many farmers headed for Mexico City or the United States in search of jobs. Mexico began to import maize from the United States.

Later, when the 1982 debt crisis caused the cancellation of the construction projects where they were largely employed, Chiapan farmers were forced back to farming, and they had to intensify and diversify crops such as maize or coffee, which meant investment in farm chemicals and taking on risks with bank loans. The unequal financial resources available to them intensified the pattern of uneven development in rural Mexico and widened the already existing gap between rich and poor in peasant communities. If that were not enough, when world oil prices plummeted in 1986, the government cut the subsidies it had offered during the previous decade.

THE DEBT-DRIVEN economic crisis was in part provoked by the collision between high-expenditure government programs and the reality of international market forces and structural adjustment (Fox 1994, 247). The state began to withdraw from its regulatory role, and the market protection offered to the peasant economy gradually disappeared over the course of the 1980s. The retreat of the state in some cases is necessary to allow building social capital, according to Theda Skocpol (1995). Intense peasant mobilizations then brought on a subsequent backlash by political and economic elites with brutal repression in some parts of Mexico, such as Juchitán, Oaxaca (Fox 1996).

The 1980s and 1990s: Neoliberal Reforms and the Restructuring of the State

The role of the state changed with the introduction of so-called neoliberal economic policies after the 1982 economic crisis. Neoliberalism is an ideology that gives a central role to market forces in development, and its supporters believe that the state must be shrunk to minimize its "interference" in the market. The budget-cutting and free market policies of neoliberalism were imposed on Mexico (and most other Third World countries) by the World Bank, International Monetary Fund, and the U.S. government, as a condition for debt restructuring under what is called "structural adjustment" (Otero 2004). Never again was the state to generously spread financing around peasant Mexico. There was to be less state support, and what was left was to be more selectively given out.

The government of Carlos Salinas de Gortari (1988–94) promoted private sector–led economic development while at the same time trying to keep rural areas under state control. His government implemented more targeted distributive policies, trying to be more efficient in redistribution, as the solution to the rural crisis. The backbone of the Salinas program focused on marketing, infrastructure, and services rather than on productive projects. Thus, the government retreated and left production in the hands of the producers themselves. All the organizations that were engaged with governmental institutions in productive projects had to restructure their efforts in accordance with the new conditions or run the risk of disappearing.

By the end of the decade, most of the state agricultural agencies, including INMECAFE, were privatized or cut back sharply as part of structural adjustment. This had serious consequences for small farmers, particularly those in remote areas like the Lacandón jungle in Chiapas, where small coffee growers had depended on INMECAFE for technical assistance, credit, and subsidized transport and processing (Collier 1999).

Peasant Organizations Change the Way They Work

The withdrawal of government support, the privatization of institutions, and low market prices for their products formed the framework in which campesinos throughout Mexico were forced to reconfigure their activities. They had to confront their new, more intense condition of marginality in a more globalized context. The overall response of the campesino sector to the reduction of the state sector was threefold. First, organizations across Mexico with very different objectives (land reform, agricultural supports, workers' rights, etc.) began to coordinate with each other, to some extent addressing long-standing divisions on the Mexican Left (Foley 1991, 59). Second, the national campesino organizations shifted toward more politically independent positions (e.g., independent from "official" organizations affiliated with the PRI and other political parties) and began building more plural memberships as the density of their networks expanded rapidly (Putnam 1993). Some of the important organizations included the Plan de Ayala National Coalition (CNPA),[2] the Peasant and Farmworker Independent Union (CIOAC),[3] and the National United Autonomous Campesino Organizations (UNORCA).[4] The CIOAC, for example, organized in Chiapas and attracted coffee farmers with projects oriented toward production; the new organization emphasized a willingness to work with other groups, including even the officialist National

Campesino Association (CNC). UNORCA promoted the organization and unity of peasants to put pressure on state institutions to obtain credit and inputs. Finally, peasant organizations tended to become more development oriented as they took on productive projects and developed skills in negotiating with the state and navigating the market.

Two distinct but interlinked sets of demands from campesino organizations took shape during the 1980s. The first set of demands was derived from the continued struggle for land (agrarian demands) together with farm workers' demands for better working conditions and higher salaries (labor demands). Organizations that focused on these demands were more political in their outlook and strategy. In the 1980s a second set of demands came from campesinos who had already won access to land and now sought support to produce on that land (agricultural demands). Some agrarian movements incorporated so as to become legally able to receive bank credit and thus obtain resources in the form of credit and support for their production practices. Typical organizations pursued both lines of struggle for some time, though later they began to separate again into groups that pursued specific struggles.

The objective of the groups with more agricultural demands was known as "appropriation of the production process"—meaning they would control all stages of the production, processing, and marketing of their products (Bartra 1999; Celis et al. 1991; Fox 1994). Instead of relying on state extension agents for technical assistance, or state marketing agencies for storage of harvests, organizations began to have their own agronomists, their own storage and processing facilities, and so forth. These campesino organizations shifted away from the militant tactics of their land-seeking counterparts and instead relied on nonviolent mobilizations and strategic negotiations with different official institutions to meet their demands for economic development (Fox 1994). UNORCA was formed as the merger of many regional organizations in 1985 and later gave birth to sectorally focused national networks of peasant-managed credit unions, input distributors, and maize, coffee, and lumber producers (ibid.).

When Gustavo Gordillo, a politician who advocated campesino-managed production, served as secretary of agriculture in the late 1980s, the state took on *la apropiación del proceso productivo* as its motto (Fox 1994). Coffee producer organizations were part of the agricultural demand group of organizations, and they became the most dynamic and important sector among campesino organizations during the 1980s and early 1990s. In fact, the coffee sector became one of the most successful examples of production managed by peasant organizations. It was during this period that the state offered the most support to this sector, focusing on peasant organizations rather than on the coffee sector as a whole. As a result, new organizations emerged and older ones were transformed.

Among the many new coffee cooperatives formed in Mexico in this period were CEPCO (State Coordinator of Coffee Producers of Oaxaca), UCIRI (Union of Indigenous Communities of the Isthmus Region), UPCV (Union of Coffee Producers of Veracruz), UCIZONI (Union of Indigenous Communities of the Northern Sierra of the Isthmus), CARTT (*Tosepan Titataniske* ["we shall overcome" in Nahuátl] Regional Agricultural Cooperative of the Northern Sierra of Puebla), Union Majomut (Union of Ejidos and Indigenous Communities of Majomut), and ISMAM (Indígenas de la Sierra Madre de Motozintla).

Struggles over land and the improvement of working conditions led to the convergence of campesino networks statewide and, later, nationally. The high level of social effervescence in the early 1980s was evidenced by the abundance of popular political materials published, in very accessible language, by organizations (both church and political groups) during this period (Taller de Análisis 1988, nd; Velasco 1988; Diócesis de Chiapas 1981). Campesino organizations in Chiapas with agrarian demands established connections and links of support with national peasant organizations like the Central Independiente de Obreros Agrícolas y Campesinos (CIOAC) in the area of Simojovel, and Línea Proletaria, a more politically sectarian political organization. These organizations promoted self-managed productive projects to obtain credit and support from the government, mainly in the northern and jungle regions (Taller de Análisis 1988).

Changes in the Coffee Sector

In 1989, because of the breakup of the International Coffee Agreement, the international price of coffee fell below the high cost of production of technified coffee. Many large and medium-sized technified growers went bankrupt, and the banks repossessed their land, machinery, and processing plants. Some of the largest growers, who could make their payments because they had access to outside sources of capital, survived. However, in Chiapas, at least, most of the mid-size technified farmers were foreclosed (Meda 1995). Conversely, organic farmers survived the crisis, as the price of organic coffee never dropped significantly. Peasants using traditional technology lost substantial income, but unlike those who produced technified coffee, prices for them never actually fell below their production costs, which are extremely low.

In response to the fall of prices, huge mobilizations targeting the pricing and transport policies of INMECAFE began to unite small producers all over Mexico. Having the same target led to unity and to the 1988 formation of the independent National Council of Coffee Organizations (CNOC) (García 1991; Hernández 1991). In Chiapas after the institutional breakdown of INMECAFE began, a statewide forum on coffee was organized and, as a result, the Consejo Estatal de Cafeticultura was founded in October 1992 to lobby with regard to sectoral policies (Salazar 1993). The Consejo had representatives from all coffee sectors including small, medium, and large farmers. The differences in power among them led to a predominance of the largest producers, driving small farmers to join CNOC and to create a CNOC chapter in Chiapas. The social capital built up in Chiapas allowed many organizations to survive the crash in coffee prices by converting to organic methods and by taking advantage of fair trade opportunities. Nonetheless, the crisis of coffee in Chiapas also helped fuel the Zapatista rebellion, as part of the Zapatista social base consisted of these same indigenous coffee growers, who were initially left out of the reconfigured coffee market, thanks to the privatization of INMECAFE (Collier 1994).

The Zapatista Rebellion and Resurgent Ethnic Identity

On January 1, 1994, the day the North American Free Trade Agreement (NAFTA) went into effect, the Zapatista National Liberation Army (EZLN) rose up and declared war on the Mexican government. After only twelve days of armed combat in several regions of Chiapas, the federal government was forced to declare a cease-fire, due to pressure from a widespread mobilization of national and international civil society—demonstrating more clearly than ever the importance of civil society—and in order to avoid a crisis in investor confidence in a national economy that increasingly depended on foreign investment.

The EZLN was forged in communities of colonists in the remote jungle area, on the poor rainforest soils found there. A new sort of community had been taking shape in Eastern Chiapas, in the isolated settlements of the Lacandón jungle (Martinez-Torres 2001). These communities were different both from the mestizo[5] communities in other parts of Mexico, from which some had come, and from the Chiapas highlands, from which the indigenous majority came. The latter were no longer in monolingual or bilingual (Tzotzil/Spanish, Tojolabal/Spanish, etc.) villages, but rather mixed together with indigenous people of different language groups and with mestizos as well. As for the mestizos, they found themselves living with indigenous people. All faced the same enemies: cattle ranchers, forest rangers, corrupt bureaucrats, poor soils, and declining prices. Displaced peoples, driven from their places of origin by diverse manifestations of capitalism and Mexican government policies, joined in a struggle for survival against perceived injustices. In this process they gave *indigenousness* new importance, adding mestizo as yet another ethnic category. Running contrary to a global trend toward ethnic conflict, the Zapatistas proved to be inclusive rather than exclusive.

This happens in many places around the world as local people respond to the deepening globalization of the economy, which drives them from "exploitation to irrelevance" (Castells 1997). We find identity-based responses to neoliberal restructuring emerging from grassroots organizations all over the world, especially in indigenous areas. New pan-indigenous movements—or what Bretón (2002) calls *neo-indigenismo*—across Latin America call for autonomy, self-definition of group identity along cultural and ethnic lines, and the use of old and new strategies of contestation (Benjamin 1995; Black 1998; Caudillo 1998; Peña 1998).

In this context, Collier (1999) documents the reconfiguration of class and ethnicity brought about by economic restructuring in Chiapas, highlighting the emergence of a new pan-indigenous identity. The new, broad group identity as Mayas has helped greatly in building solidarity and a sense of common purpose (in building social capital) inside many organizations. Some of the coffee cooperatives studied here are relatively successful organizations that were built using, at least in part, Mayan ethnic identity as a source of social cohesion.

The EZLN organizing took place in nearly complete isolation and, although there were internal differences concerning whether or not to take up arms, the level of trust and loyalty in indigenous communities—thanks to the norms and social relations that generate a sense of mutual obligation within these communities—was such that nobody denounced the preparations for rebellion. This armed uprising provoked a split within the elite over whether to respond with repression or with negotiation, and that split led to a cease-fire. A web of external allies was formed immediately afterward, which then helped sustain the very existence of the Zapatista movement while protecting it from government repression.

The mobilization in Chiapas had a powerful echo across Mexico and internationally and shook up Mexican elites and the state alike, generating a new terrain of political opportunity in which Mexican civil society voted the seventy-year dominance of power by the Revolutionary Institutional Party (PRI) out of the presidency a few years later. Peace talks started that same year and have continued intermittently until today. In the meantime, paramilitary groups became active in a low-intensity conflict that the people of Chiapas have had to confront ever since. As part of the state's low-intensity conflict, Chiapas has been inundated with funds for development projects. These have provoked many divisions within and among communities and organizations inside and outside the conflict zone.

On the one hand, the Zapatistas have made clear their intention to build political and economic autonomy without government funds; on the other hand, the state continues to be the main source of funds for peasant organizations. The political stance of each organization has thus become a critical feature, because they must either come down on one side or the other or choose to remain in an ambiguous gray zone. The state has offered many inducements to organizations that distance themselves from the Zapatistas and, before the change of presidents, allied themselves with the main political party, the PRI, or other structures of power. In the late 1990s both the federal and state governments were, for the first time ever, willing to support peasant organizations affiliated with other political parties, as long as their members did not become Zapatistas.

Nevertheless, some alliances were formed in the other direction, as communities chose to join with the Zapatistas in search of autonomy, land, and dignity. As the Zapatistas receive significant support from the international solidarity movement, these organizations and communities might forgo opportunities for alliance with the state, but they could gain the opportunities from the alliance with international external actors. The Zapatista movement increased the global name recognition of Chiapas, and that has helped market the coffee of the small-scale producers from this state. In fact, the 1994 jump in coffee prices in Chiapas was attributed to the Zapatistas. The international allies of this movement opened up new solidarity markets that the first Zapatista coffee co-op was to benefit from.

Chapter 6

Sustainable Development
Building Social and Natural Capital

THE CENTRAL PROPOSITION of this book is that the formation or accumulation of social capital can combine with strategies based on investments in natural capital to produce positive results in terms of broad-based, sustainable development, and provide positive synergisms between them. If broad-based development is taken to mean improvements in living standards for the poorest sectors of society—like indigenous people and poor peasant farmers in Chiapas, Mexico's poorest state—then sustainable development means to do so in ways that conserve and improve productive resources like soil and biodiversity. The relative success of small-farmer coffee cooperatives in Chiapas, Mexico, can be understood in terms of their ability to achieve some of the economic and ecological goals of sustainable development, based on their mobilization of social capital and their investment in natural capital.

Sustainable development consists of goals, strategies, and processes that together provide more socially just, economically viable, and ecologically sound alternative tracks to conventional development, offering improved livelihoods to the poor in ways that promote both their empowerment and the conservation or improvement of key natural resources so that the basis of productive activities can be maintained into the future (Lele 1991; Pretty 1998). Anthony Bebbington (1997) lists a number of indicators of sustainability, among which are the reduction of out-migration, an increase of local control over economic processes, increased incomes, the use of low-external-input technology, improved resource management, diversification, and greater local economic and social linkages.

Sustainable development is a process characterized by direct and local participation and control over the "way in which people live and work," rather than a set of goals designed and implemented in a top-down fashion (Barkin 1998, 53). This process includes the redistribution and balancing of political and economic power, an emphasis on food self-sufficiency, and the interaction between natural, productive, and human systems. Broadbased rural development is linked to the rise of the economic, social, and cultural power of the peasantry (*campesinado*), and that implies a political struggle for control of the productive apparatus (Martínez Borrego 1991). Clearly, social mobilization of the population is indispensable for such a development project (see, for example, Enríquez 1997).

Especially in recent decades, as states have increasingly abandoned their roles in regulating markets and promoting rural development, a new generation of more sophisticated organizations of peasants and indigenous people has emerged across Latin America. These organizations have occupied part of the space and many of the roles vacated by the state, in order to organize their own productive activities, offer their own agricultural extension to their members, and take charge of the marketing of their own products (Fox 1994). This holds true for the case of organic and fair trade certified coffee (González and Nigh 2004). But how have these organizations achieved the success they so far have? The first essential ingredient was the formation of substantial social capital.

Cycles and Pathways of Social Capital Formation

The social capital implicit in peasant organizations evolves over time, as history moves through cycles of struggle, mobilization, and repression (see chapter 5). Jonathan Fox (1996, 1090) has identified these recursive cycles of contention between the state, campesino organizations and their allies (either reformers within the state or other members of civil society), and authoritarian elites, as a central characteristic of social formation in rural Mexico.

A cycle of social capital formation starts with an event such as an economic crisis, war, popular protest, or political succession. The responses of elites to the event typically has split between those whose concerns for political legitimacy lead them to seek negotiation and those who want to respond with repression. Social organizations tend to demand broader access to the state when these divisions occur, and for a time they build social capital, typically with support from external allies. Most often a given cycle closes with an authoritarian backlash, as social organizations get out of hand, and if a given organization manages to conserve its autonomy during the ensuing repression, it will use that autonomy when the next political opportunity appears. Fox observes that, in this process, "societal groups gain legitimacy and leverage at very different rates and in different bargaining arenas" (1092). Conflict and coalition building may either lead to or block the formation of social capital. The state is often heterogeneous, with some sectors promoting social capital formation while others block it, and both actions can occur at the same time. This leads to the coexistence of different patterns of state-society relations within the same nation-state.

As a result of these cycles of social capital formation over broad and diverse areas, the distribution of social capital across rural Mexico today is highly uneven. Fox (1996) has formulated a model in which geographically varying levels of preexistent social capital and levels of repression generated different subregional social capital regimes in Mexico. Fox notes that in some areas, even within the boundaries of the same state, three different regimes could exist: authoritarian clientelism, semiclientelism, or pluralist regimes. The first two types are characterized by the conditioning of access to resources, with or without repression. In a pluralist regime there is access to resources and autonomy and respect for political and ethnic diversity. Table 6.1 displays the regimes found in different areas of rural Mexico. The case of Chiapas in the last decade is a good example of what to expect under high levels of both social capital and repression.

Taking empirical data from case studies in rural Mexico, Fox defines three pathways to social capital development under authoritarian rule. He finds that when social organizations managed to come out of these cycles and consolidate themselves, they followed one or more of the three paths. The first, which Fox calls "state-society convergence," may take place

TABLE 6.1

Model of social capital regimes in rural Mexico

Level of repression	Level of social capital
	low
high	After a failed social challenge: demobilization. *Huasteca, Zongolica, Mixteca, Raramuri*
low	Authoritarian rule not challenged: no repression. *Mazateca, Michoacan*
	medium
high	Authoritarian rule challenged: repression fuels social energy. *Chiapas, Istmo, Huasteca, Pinotepa*
low	Semiclientelistic regime. Society-State competition: more negotiation less coercion. *Juchitan, Mazateca*
	high
high	Dual political power: mobilization vs. authoritarian rule. *Zapatista controled zone*
low	Pluralist enclaves resulted from previous successful mobilizations. *Yaqui, Purepecha*

Source: Slightly modified from Fox 1996, 1093–94

when an opening at the top (in the state) is filled from below (society). This path is characterized by cooperation between state reformists and the local societal organizations that survived the previous cycles. Typically, middle- and lower-level reformists from the state agencies recognize and support societal organizations.[1] The organizations vary in their responses, due to their different political strategies or capacity to take advantage of these openings. When taking advantage of an opening, a participatory process occurs, to the point of some transfer of state authority to representative organizations. Later, a form of state coercion closes this cycle. In the coffee sector of Chiapas, the Unión de Uniones was formed during the 1970s when the first opening appeared via programs of state support for peasant enterprises. It was transformed over the course of following cycles, eventually giving rise to the Unión de Ejidos de la Selva. By the 1990s some of its members had become Zapatistas and left the organization, while many others continue in La Selva. The Majomut

73

coffee cooperative began with the support of state reformists in the National Indigenous Institute (INI). These allies were crucial for the initial organizing. Communities with different political allegiances were part of Majomut from the beginning, and today Majomut is tolerant of diverse political affiliations and religious practices. This quality has given the organization strength. The Unión de Crédito Pajal Yakaltik was formed in the cycle of the 1980s and later split into several new organizations, including the Tzotzilotic Tzobolotic cooperative. Half the members of this latter organization subsequently became Zapatistas and left the organization in the 1990s, giving birth to the quintessential 1990s cycle organization, MutVitz (for greater detail on coffee producer organizations in Chiapas, see chapter 7).

Fox's second pathway, "collaboration between local and external civil society organizations," occurs in regions where the authoritarian state does not allow for an opening from above. In the absence of such an opening, opportunities are opened by local civil society elements allied with other external societal actors. Churches, NGOs, and human rights groups can all act as allies to open spaces where civil society can participate and, at the same time, buffer it from potential repression from the state. In this regard, Robert Putnam (1993) and Mark Granovetter (1973) argue that the relationships established outside the community ("weak" ties) are most important for development, because they allow outside connections, solidarity, and new information to be brought into consideration. In the same line, Ross Gittell and Avis Vidal (1998) believe that broader, extracommunity ties that cross social divides, which are referred to as "bridging" social capital, prevent the pursuit of narrow interests. Environmental, development, church-led, and democratic programs and projects may all help in the formation of local social capital. This multiplicity of factors can generate a greater "density" of networks (Putnam 1993).[2] However, while Fox highlights the importance of these alliances in buffering against negative sanctions, he also mentions the risk of inducing "subordinate semi-clientelism, without actually engendering a thickening of civil society" (1096).

Among the Chiapas coffee co-ops, ISMAM was formed with religious allies who were looking for economic alternatives for their faithful. A key individual was a priest-advisor who provided leadership by working alongside the cooperative members. They have achieved a significant scale that allows them to buffer repression, and they are run quite democratically.

Fox describes the third path as an "independent production of social capital from below." It is characterized by the formation of social capital with no external allies present in the initial stages, which is later supported by networks of civil society. For Fox, the Zapatista National Liberation Army (EZLN) is a quintessential example of this pathway. The internal ties that created a sense of mutual obligation inside the Zapatista communities were such that nobody revealed the preparations for the uprising. The MutVitz coffee co-op is made up of Zapatista supporters, and was created in the cycle of the 1990s, supported by the international solidarity movement in support of the Zapatistas. Their success is building as they take advantage of solidarity markets. They are a result of both the independent production of social capital and of the support of external allies.

Loyalty and Ethnic Identity in Coffee Cooperatives

James Coleman (1988) has defined social capital as those aspects of social structure that facilitate actions of individuals who are part of the same social structure, namely social relations and norms. Here social capital varies depending on group membership and social circumstance. According to Coleman, a sense of obligation is created through social norms and the social relations through which information is passed, and that obligation is enforced through social sanctions. Calling in the obligation of others can reduce the costs of production for individuals and families and can make possible goals that would otherwise be impossible. This sense of obligation functions as a form of insurance and is one part of the social assets of an individual or family. In the case of coffee cooperatives in Chiapas, the price fluctuation cycles of the coffee market can place stress on this form of social capital. When prices are low, all members are happy to have an organization buy from them, yet when prices are high there is a great temptation for members to sell to intermediaries (coyotes), who will pay cash long before the organizational representative arrives to receive the harvest. In such a situation, it is quite important that the social capital within an organization be strong enough to enforce loyalty.[3]

One key attribute that organizations of indigenous people often use to promote their local development initiatives and/or larger societal reforms is their ethnic identity, which can act as a social glue that strengthens their social capital (Hart 1997; Bretón 2002). For example, the new organizational structures formed in Chiapas in the 1970s and 1980s mediated a transformation from largely kinship-based forms of organization in indigenous communities, toward more production-oriented structures. However, Antonio López Meza (1996) observes that these organizations were able to exhibit effective decision making only to the extent that they incorporated traditional practices from indigenous cultures of consensus-based decision making and respect for traditional authorities within their operational mechanisms.

Monica de Hart (1997) proposes the term *ethnic development,* in which the goals of organizations are related to mainstream development discourses of improving living standards but reformulate such discourses based on dynamic notions of cultural and ethnic identity. The point here is that their demands echo some of the goals of traditional development, like potable water and electrification, yet reject its top-down methods. Such grassroots development initiative accepts participation in the global market as a necessary component, taking into account market demands such as quality control, efficiency, and administration and market limitations like overreliance on agricultural exports. Ethnic development uses the ties that bind people together in networks of reciprocity and trust based on a perceived common ethnic and cultural identity—what we might call ethnic social capital—to demand a reformulation of the terms of participation in the global economy. Indigenous organizations demand a collective rather than an individual participation, maintaining autonomy while also having direct contact with external participants and markets, without mediation by the state. Hart argues that ethnic identity permits a new kind of insertion in the market on more favorable terms.

This restated ethnic identity among some of the organizations of indigenous coffee farmers in Chiapas is a form of generating social capital that can contribute to sustainable development. Thus, a number of the coffee grower organizations are built around ethnic identity, which helps build internal cohesion and serves as a marketing hook in the world market as their products are marketed as "organic coffee grown by indigenous people in Chiapas" (Hernández and Nigh 1998).

Social and Natural Capital

Paul Winters and colleagues (2001) argue, on the basis of case studies in Mexico and other Latin American countries, that social capital is a key factor in the sustainability of rural development. In a similar vein, two groups of researchers showed that the accumulation of sufficient social capital was key to the success of networks for exchange of native seeds (Badstue et al. 2002) and for community forest management practices in Mexico (Bray et al. 2003). All these cases also involve the management of natural capital, such as seeds and forests, and while most analysts have tended to separate the concepts of social capital from those of natural capital,[4] recently a few scholars have highlighted the interrelatedness of social and natural capital in sustainable development (Pretty 1997, 1998; Boyce and Pastor 2001).

James Boyce and Manuel Pastor affirm that the formation of social capital and the building of, or investing in, natural capital are undeniably linked. Natural capital, or natural assets, include "the land on which we live and grow our food and fiber; the water we drink and use to irrigate crops, generate electricity, and dispose of wastes; the air we breathe, into which we also emit wastes; the fish in the ocean and the trees in the forest; other animals and plants, both wild and domesticated; the atmosphere that envelops our planet; the ores, minerals, and fossil fuels beneath the Earth's surface; and the solar energy that powers the biosphere. In short, natural assets are the wealth on which human well-being—and survival itself—ultimately depend" (2001, 3). In the context of small-scale coffee producers in Chiapas, the social capital they had accumulated in their organizations and networks was critical to surviving the reconfiguration of the global coffee market, and in being able to take advantage of new niches in the market, like those for organic, fair trade, and Zapatista coffee. In the case of organic coffee, the building up of soil fertility with successive applications of compost, the management of shade diversity, and other improvements are investments in their natural capital or assets. But it was the organizations and networks (social capital) that allowed farmers to get certified as organic producers and receive a price premium, and their organizations provided them with critical technical assistance in the technological transition.

The term *natural capital* entered widespread usage with the work of environmental economists David Pearce and R. Kerry Turner (1990). For them, natural capital is a complex category that performs three distinct environmental functions: provision of resources for production (raw materials), absorption of wastes from production (either positively, as recycling or fertilizing, or negatively, as polluting or eroding), and environmental services (like tree cover that moderates climate, or watersheds that provide drinking water). In 1992 the term was linked to the concept of sustainability (Jansson et al. 1994).

Thomas Prugh and colleagues (1999) recognize three major types of natural capital: *renewable* natural capital, which continuously maintains and regenerates itself when left alone; *nonrenewable* natural capital, mostly in the form of mineral deposits and fossil fuel; and *cultivated* natural capital, which encompasses all agricultural and aquacultural systems, including tree farms, sod farms, fish ponds, greenhouses, and nurseries. Rayen Quiroga (1999, 3) defines natural capital as the set of "natural dynamics" that form and regenerate natural resources that provide humans with environmental services. According to Mathis Wackernagel and William Rees (1997), natural capital consists of the *natural assets* capable of producing sustainable flows of energy, defined in the broadest sense. More than an inventory of resources, natural capital includes all the components of the ecosphere and the relationships among them. In this light, natural capital, or natural assets, include both sources and sinks of materials that are part of a natural process. Sources are stocks of renewable and nonrenewable raw materials, including land, forests, fisheries, and mineral deposits. Sinks are resources such as air, water, and soil that have the capacity to absorb and decompose those materials—including wastes from human production and consumption.

This trend in thinking links natural-asset-building strategies with poverty reduction. Boyce and Pastor argue that beyond better incomes, the poor need more assets: "natural assets, along with other assets, like financial wealth and community organization [social capital], can be part of a comprehensive strategy to reduce poverty and empower communities" (2001, 2). They argue that building the natural assets of communities can be an effective part of poverty reduction and environmental protection. They lay out four routes to the building of natural assets (Boyce and Pastor 2001 and Boyce and Shelley 2003):

1. *Investment in natural capital.* Natural capital can be increased or diminished by human activity—natural capital to be degraded, depreciated,

or depleted (Prugh et al. 1999)—therefore it is possible to consciously invest in building it up. Boyce and Pastor argue that investments that maintain or increase stocks of natural capital help reduce poverty and protect the environment. Such investments can be made with public and philanthropic resources, or they can be made by the poor people themselves. For example, soil and water conservation investments can be targeted to reduce what Anil Agarwal (1992) calls "ecological poverty," which occurs when the livelihoods of communities in marginal rural areas are constrained by the impoverishment of the natural resources they depend on. In the case of small farmers, investments in natural capital might include soil conservation, soil restoration, or soil-building activities (terracing, composting, addition of manure) as well as biodiversity enhancement (mixed cropping, use of diverse shade species, integration of crops and animals). These activities involve the technological options small-scale farmers normally would use in their agricultural practices.

2. *Redistribution or democratizing access.* This strategy implies the redistribution of, or access to, natural assets, especially nonrenewable resources like land and minerals, and therefore it is controversial and politically contentious. Land reform programs are rare around the globe, but they have proven to be one of the best sources of economic growth and poverty reduction, as in East Asia (Rosset 2001). The access of small coffee growers in Mexico to productive land and security of land tenure is largely due to earlier periods of land redistribution and the creation of ejidos and other forms of communal land tenure.

3. *Internalization.* Dominant models of economic development, including the World Bank projects discussed by von Amsberg (2001), tend to externalize the environmental costs of its activities so that society at large, rather than the firm or the project, must bear the costs of pollution and the depletion and degradation of resources. If these costs were to be internalized by the companies that produced them, the balances might well look considerably less positive. In the same way, some activities of poor people actually produce external benefits for society at large, and these are sometimes referred to as environmental services. Small-scale farmers, as well as larger growers, may, for example, protect the water supply of urban areas by responsibly managing watersheds, or they may support future agriculture by conserving genetic crop resources in the form of local varieties they plant. Boyce and Pastor suggest that "making

79

sure that the poor are paid for the benefits their resource management provides to others" and that internalizing the external benefits "would strengthen their livelihoods and their incentives to continue providing these services." We might imagine government subsidies for conversion to organic in the case of farming (as has been done in Europe and Costa Rica). There is also the concrete example of society paying a premium for certified organic products, like coffee, on the assumption that such a production practice contributes to the preservation of the environment.

4. *Sharing the commons, or appropriating open-access resources.* Sharing the commons refers to open-access resources, like air or oceans, that "in theory are freely available to all, but in practice are available only to those with the ability to claim them" (Boyce and Shelley 2003). For example, public forest lands may often be treated as open-access resources, which anyone, or at least anyone able to pay a bribe, can clear-cut. Local residents and forest dwellers may lose out in the scramble of such competition. Converting them to common-property regimes, like ejidos, where community rules govern resource management, can strengthen local peoples' claims and access, and lead to more sustainable resource use.

In this context, coffee farmers in Chiapas have participated in the building of natural assets or natural capital by intensifying their production with organic methods and internalizing some of the benefits via a price premium for certification.

However, there are important criticisms concerning the use of words like *capital* or *assets* to describe nature. For example, the concept of natural capital can be co-opted by dominant groups and institutions like the World Bank to legitimize the privatization and commodification of nature,[5] and its control through market mechanisms, as in the case of patented seeds or the purchase of carbon emission rights (e.g., World Bank 1997).

Writing as a World Bank country director for the Philippines, Joachim von Amsberg (2001) has warned that since the bank's projects tend to treat natural assets as cost-free inputs, they run the risk of faulty cost-benefit analyses that fail to take into account the costs of depleted oil reserves, degraded soils, lost biodiversity, and polluted air and water. He argues that, were natural capital to be taken fully into account, the bank's project evaluations might often lead to very different and less positive conclusions.

Martin O'Connor (1994) argues that capital is now in a new, "ecological" stage, in which nature is seen as a commodity. He asserts that this is a "semiotic conquest of the planet," where everything, even our genes, come under the code of production, an economic vision, and the laws of value, in which absolutely everything is mediated by monetary signs. In the research presented in this book, the term *natural capital* is not used to refer to the privatization of nature, nor is *social capital* used in reference to the commercialization of human social relations. Here, I use *natural capital* to highlight the importance of nature to local economies and communities, and the risks they face when it is degraded. In the same way, *social capital* is used to stress the importance of organization and networks in effective community and regional development. In the context of development, these two terms are meant to draw attention to the need for making better and more sustainable investments.

As we have observed, the management of an agricultural system involves the management of natural capital, and the intensification of agriculture is the investment of labor and resources in making that natural capital more productive. In fact, for many decades the notion of intensifying agriculture has been understood as the basis for rural development and as a key step in the solution to poverty. Thus one of the most important contemporary debates in rural development circles concerns the intensification of agriculture.[6]

Two Routes to the Intensification of Agriculture

The two principal positions in this debate are represented by the differences between the two main approaches to intensification. One perspective posits that increased agricultural output can be achieved only by using so-called *science-based,* or "modern," agriculture. In recognizing the mistakes of the first Green Revolution, this school proposes a "second green revolution" targeted at poorer, more marginal farmers (Borlaug 1992, 1994; Paarlberg 1994). The intention is to bring modern technology to bear on small-farmer agriculture: improved seed varieties, monoculture, chemical fertilizer, pesticides, and perhaps genetic engineering.

The contrasting approach, is the *sustainable intensification* of agriculture (Pretty 1997), based on investment in and enhancement of natural capital. Empirical evidence shows that much highly productive agriculture around the world uses low-input and regenerative techniques (Altieri 1995, 1996, 1999; Hazell 1995; Hewitt and Smith 1995; Pretty 1995a,b; Reijntjes, Haverkort, and Waters-Bayer 1996). The sustainable intensification of agriculture affirms that it is possible to achieve substantial growth in productivity, in currently unimproved or degraded areas, while at the same time protecting or even regenerating natural capital by using agroecological techniques (see also D. Carruthers 1995; UNDP 1995). These techniques include breaking up the monoculture structure of agricultural systems by introducing mixed cropping and by integrating crops and livestock, as well as by the use of natural predators, local materials to prepare compost, and functional biodiversity to improve system performance (like regulated shade in coffee culture). This approach also relies on the creativity, knowledge, and ability of individual farmers to design their own experiments as they seek better results (Altieri 1995; Pretty 1999; Rosset and Altieri 1997).

An important caveat is that for rural development to succeed, regardless of which technology or route to intensification is followed, peasant farmers must have adequate access to quality land and other productive resources, to farm credit to finance their production, and to markets that provided decent prices for their products (De Janvry and Sadoulet 2004). In no case have peasant families achieved such conditions without engaging in constant struggle through their local, regional, or national organizations and movements.

THE TERM *sustainable agriculture,* of which organic farming may be thought of as an example (Pretty 1997, 1999), represents, in part, a reaction by civil society to fifty years of agricultural and rural development policies focused on the first kind of intensification of agriculture. That "science-based" intensification requires the use of external inputs like chemical pesticides and fertilizers, machines, and large-scale irrigation to boost food production. This technology generates economic concentration; social exclusion; the rise of expensive, patented "improved" seeds; the depreciation of natural capital via compacted, eroded, and degraded soils; the loss of biodiversity; the pollution of groundwater; and other negative consequences (Pretty 1995a,b; Pretty, Morison, and Hine 2003; Rosset and Altieri 1997). In fact, in many agricultural areas the degradation of productive resources like soils threatens the future sustainability of production. While some researchers (e.g., Avery 1995) argue that organic farming is the opposite of intensification, leading inevitably to lower yields, Pretty (1997) responds that there are many low-external-input techniques that nevertheless represent net intensification or greater productivity per unit area.

Both routes to intensification are apparent among the coffee producers in Chiapas. One subset of small-scale coffee farmers uses agrochemicals to boost coffee yields, while another subset have adopted a series of organic, more agroecological techniques, based on investment in and improvement of their natural capital—what we might call cultivated natural capital. Social capital plays a key role in their having been able to do so. In the following chapters, I will take a closer look at the coffee cooperatives in Chiapas, with an eye to detecting the key elements and outcomes of the production of organic coffee that many of them are involved in.

Chapter 7

A Study of Coffee Cooperatives in Chiapas

THE ORGANIZATIONS FORMED by small-scale coffee producers are part of the strategies that campesinos and indigenous people have used to negotiate their economic, political, and social position in the changing terrain of this period of neoliberal reforms. Compared to the organizations of peasants who produce other commodities, the organizations of small coffee farmers have been remarkably successful at entering the global market. In Chiapas, indigenous families are the main producers of organic coffee, and they have helped make Mexico into the leading producer of organic coffee in the world.

Chapters 7, 8, and 9 delve more deeply into the coffee cooperatives of Chiapas and the production technologies they have employed over the past two decades. I focus on understanding the organizational, technological, spatial, and family-level dimensions of the ongoing organic coffee boom. These chapters are based on a socioeconomic and ecological survey I administered to families of small coffee farmers stratified across different geographic regions of Chiapas and by membership in different coffee grower organizations. I also gathered ecological data by visiting the family's coffee groves and taking measurements. Complementary data on the history of the organizations were gathered through interviews with key individuals and from reviews of the literature, government documents, and relevant news media.

The research covers all of the principal coffee-producing regions of Chiapas, and the fieldwork was conducted between 1996 and 2000. Doing the fieldwork over several years allowed me to observe the changing nature of the coffee cycle from the farmers' point of view and to monitor how coffee organizations adjust each year to changing prices and conditions. The 150 families surveyed in this study belong to six major organizations of small coffee farmers and to several smaller ones. The organizations were chosen to be representative of the larger variation among all such organizations in terms of their technology strategy (do they promote organic farming? are their members mostly chemical producers?), their ethnic identification (does the organization represent itself to its members and to society as "indigenous"?), and their political affiliation (are they pro-Zapatista? are they aligned with the government? are they independent?) (see table 7.1).

The Families Interviewed

The families that participated in this study come from thirty-six communities located over the rich biodiversity and multiple microclimates of the coffee-producing regions of Chiapas (see map 7.1). The greatest number of participants are from the ethnically diverse western and eastern highlands (Los Altos). Mayan Tzotzil and Tzeltal participant families from the eastern highlands live in seven communities located in the municipalities[1] of Chenalho and Tenejapa. The western highlands participants were drawn from six Tzotzil communities distributed between the municipalities of El Bosque and San Andres Larrainzar. From the northern region, Tzeltal and Chol families from five communities located near Ocosingo City and the municipality of Chilon participated in this study.

The families interviewed from the jungle come from eight communities, mainly located in the municipality of Las Margaritas and in the southeastern part of the municipality of Ocosingo. They are mixed indigenous and mestizo families who colonized the area within the past five decades. In the very steep sierra region three communities from two municipalities around the town of Motozintla were visited. The sierra region families are mostly descendants of Mayan Mam with only a few elders speaking the language. In the Soconusco region, the participants come from seven

85

TABLE 7.1.
Key characteristics in 2000 of the organizations studied

Organization	Technological focus				Ethnic identification			Political stance		
	Organic	Natural	Chemical	Transition	Indigenous	Mixed	Mestizo	ProEZLN	ProPRI	Independent/ atonomous
ISMAM	x	-	-	x	x	x	-	-	-	x
Lázaro Cárdenas	-	-	x	-	-	-	x	-	x	-
La Selva	x	x	-	x	x	x	-	-	-	x
Majomut	x	x	-	x	x	-	-	x	-	x
MutVitz	-	-	x	x	x	-	-	x	-	-
Tzotzilotic	-	x	x	-	-	x	-	-	-	x
Other orgs.	x	x	x	x	-	x	-	-	x	x

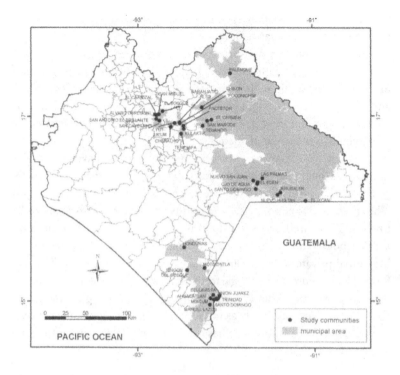

Map 7.1. Study areas in Chiapas

communities in three municipalities. All of the participants in the
Soconusco are Spanish-speaking *mestizo* families, mainly descendants from
Guatemalan indigenous people, and a few families have Chinese ancestry
as well. The research covered four communities located on the slopes of
the highest mountain in the region, the Tacana volcano (4,060 meters).

The participants belonging to the *ISMAM* coffee cooperative live in the
Soconusco and sierra regions. Families interviewed from the *La Selva*
cooperative live in the jungle and in the northern regions. The *Lázaro
Cárdenas* cooperative families are all from the Soconusco. Families interviewed belonging to the *Majomut* cooperative live in the eastern and
western highlands. Members of the recently formed *MutVitz* coffee cooperative live in the western highlands, as do those from the *Tzotzilotic
Tzobolotic* cooperative. Tzotzil, Tzeltal, and mestizo families interviewed
from the highlands, jungle, Soconusco, and northern regions, members of

several smaller organizations, and some independent producers were also interviewed for comparative purposes.

The average number of children for all the families interviewed is 5.24. The families present a three-level demographic distribution: 30.7 percent of the families have more than six children; 37 percent have between four and six children; and 30 percent have between one and three children. The remaining 3 percent have no children. An important characteristic of these families is that all of them have access to land: 27 percent of the families have less than two hectares, and 37 percent have two to four hectares. In total, sixty-four of the participants have less than five hectares; 21 percent have from five to nine hectares, and 16 percent more than ten. The access to this natural asset was mostly obtained through social mobilization. There are four different forms of land tenure: 56 percent of the families hold ejido tenure; 25 percent communal tenure; 9 percent hold individual private property, and 10 percent have co-property. This last form of land tenure is a new legal form established by the government after 1994, as a way to distribute land to small groups of people on a private basis, rather than collectively as in the case of ejido. The number of years families have held the land also has resulted in different patterns of parcel size (land holding).

Size of Holdings

The typical land holdings of a peasant family in Chiapas are made up of a series of parcels located in different parts of their communities, sometimes as much as a one- or two-hour walk apart. The farmers move mainly by foot from one parcel to another. The land holdings of families interviewed for this study vary greatly between regions. The areas with poorer soils (jungle and sierra) and more recent colonization (jungle) are where one finds the largest average holdings (figure 7.1). Families from these areas have not divided their original land grant among their children; they still work it together. In the Margaritas jungle, each family received 20 hectares during the 1970s. The sierra families received around the same from confiscated coffee fincas.

In terms of the relationship between the coffee farming technologies found (natural, transitional, organic, and chemical) and land holding (figure 7.2), it is important to point out that all technologies were found on all sizes of land holdings (among the population interviewed for this study). Natural and transitional technologies were found on similar percentages of small, medium-size, and large holdings. Transitional technology has a bit more presence among producers with 1 to 1.6 hectares than

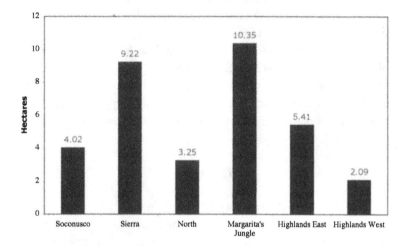

Figure 7.1. Average size of landholding by region

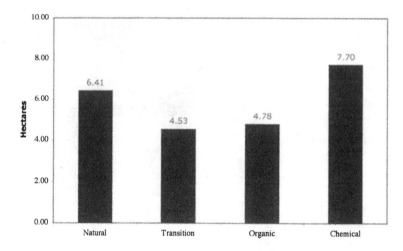

Figure 7.2. Average size of landholding by technology

does natural. Organic is most present among producers with up to 1.6 hectares. It has a medium level of presence among producers with 4 to 5 hectares and 5 to 10 hectares. Very little organic technology was found among producers with 2 to 2.75 hectares. There is very little presence of chemical technology among small producers with up to 1 hectare. The majority of the chemical technology is used by producers with 3 to 4 hectares, followed by producers with 5 to 10, with a medium presence of this technology in producers with 2 to 2.75 hectares.

The average land holding per technology is as follows: chemical technology has the largest average holdings with 7 hectares, followed by natural technology with 6 hectares (this is a surprising finding, as one might have expected the smallest producers to use this technology). The organic and transitional technologies have similar average holdings, at about 4 hectares.

Land Use

The land use patterns among the participants in this study reveal the great variety of production systems used by small-scale coffee farmers (figure 7.3). On average, less than half of the land held is used for coffee production (45 percent). A quarter is used for producing basic grains (maize and

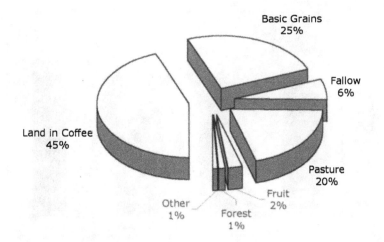

Figure 7.3. Average land use of families sampled

beans). This indicates that, on the average, small coffee producers do not depend on coffee income alone for food security, but have diversified production and produce many of their own staples. About 20 percent of their land is dedicated to pasture, reinforcing the notion that the diversity of campesino activities typically includes raising livestock. Although the practice of leaving land in fallow is disappearing, the participating small-scale coffee producers, on average, leave 6 percent of their land in fallow. A small amount of land is devoted to fruit trees (2 percent), forest reserves (1 percent), and other uses (1 percent). Monocultures of coffee are present only among those interviewed in the Soconusco region.

Organizing the families by landholding size, one can see that the families with less than 10 hectares (85 percent of the families sampled) have almost 60 percent of their land dedicated to coffee, while there are differences on the land dedicated to basic grains. Families with less than 4 hectares (64 percent of the families sampled) dedicate more of their land to basic grains than the rest of the families. This suggests that those with smaller holdings, who are likely also to be poorer, place more emphasis on food security and have more aversion to risk than do larger farmers (see table 7.2).

Organizing the data by the technology used, one can observe that the natural producers have double the area in grains as compared with those who use the other technologies. Once again, these are likelier to be poorer families, with a greater need to assure food security. If we establish a sort of continuum of intensification from natural to transitional (to organic), to organic, and finally to chemical, we find that the average hectares planted

TABLE 7.2
Average land use per holding of interviewed families

Hectares	Average landholding (all parcels)	Hectares in coffee	Hectares in basic grains	Number of parcels	Avg. altitude (meters)
Less than 2	1.16	0.71	0.79	4.02	1,351
2 to 4	3.32	2.05	1.00	3.86	1,191
5 to 9	6.62	4.04	1.67	4.49	1,084
Over 10	15.79	4.13	3.07	4.60	1,046

in coffee increases along with intensification (figure 7.4), while that in food crops declines.

Overall, there are significant average differences between organizations in terms of how the members interviewed for this study use their land, ranging from dedicating most of it to coffee, to diverse strategies including a substantial food security (growing food for home consumption) component. Part of this variability is due to regional patterns of land use that predate these organizations, while in some cases it is the result of proactive programs by organizations favoring diversification and food security. I also note that larger farmers (though still small by almost any standard) are more likely to use chemical technology, while smaller farmers are more likely to be organic or in transition to organic. This is likely due to the labor-intensive nature of organic coffee production.

Technological Change

There are various manners in which organic coffee-production technology was spread among campesinos in these coffee producer organizations. One

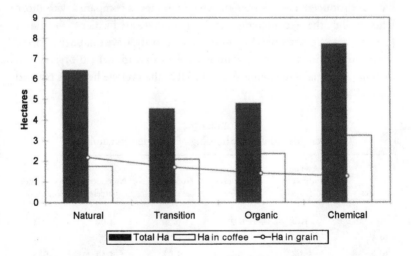

Figure 7.4. Average surface planted with coffee, basic grains, by technology (hectares per family)

of them was simply the widespread practice of following the example of others. If a coffee producer was successful in applying a technique, several neighbors would follow suit.[2] At the scale of organizations, the most successful coffee-producing organizations learned from each other. UCIRI, the Oaxacan coffee organization, learned from the first biodynamic/organic coffee farm in the world, the 300-hectare Finca Irlanda[3] in the Soconusco region. From there UCIRI went on to be the first indigenous and peasant organization in Mexico to export to alternative markets (Simpson and Rapone 1998). Since that breakthrough, all of the other organic coffee producer organizations have learned from both UCIRI and visits to Finca Irlanda. At the beginning, the practices learned were applied cookie-cutter style, exactly the way they were done in the place visited. With no or little adaptation, this had the negative effect of sometimes making farmers feel that organic was yet another externally imposed system of production (Wohlgemuth 1996). Now, after years of organic production, there is much more local experimentation and learning within each agroecological region. Still, organic methods are relatively new, and producers are in a continual learning process.

The promotion of organic production has strengthened coffee producer organizations by emphasizing working in groups and by having more advanced members serve as technical advisors for others. Almost all of the organizations are switching their technical teams from hired agronomists to farmer-technicians chosen from among their members, who give technical advice to the other members. These campesino-promoters live in the community, know the area better, and can visit the farms more regularly than can hired technicians. They also stay longer in the organization.

One particularly interesting feature of the original organic coffee organization, UCIRI, is the practice of Organized Communal Work (Trabajo Comun Organizado, or TCO). The principle of organized communal work is for the campesinos to help each other by sharing labor in the conversion to organic production. ISMAM and Majomut later implemented TCO as a way to revive and promote the tradition of communal work in indigenous communities.

Coffee producers have also benefited from the extensive research done by researchers from the *El Colegio de la Frontera Sur* (ECOSUR) research center, especially in the development of techniques to mass rear a small wasp that is a natural enemy of the coffee borer (*Hipothenemus hampei*).

ECOSUR has conducted extensive research and put out many publications about coffee production, including a series published with very accessible explanations of biological pest control techniques (Barrera, Infante, and Castillo 1996). The campesino producer organizations have also published very accessible manuals and regulations about organic production (ISMAM 1990; Majomut 1996), and at this point most small-scale coffee producers in Chiapas are using some organic techniques.

The Life Cycles of Small-Scale Coffee Producer Organizations

One finding of this research is the identification of a sort of life cycle in the coffee cooperatives, in which an organization grows, but then splits. Every organization has suffered ruptures and the separation of a part of their membership, along with some of their administrative staff and advisors.

All coffee cooperatives have a structure that includes three leadership bodies. The basic one is the general assembly, in which representatives from the communities gather to collectively make decisions. The general assembly delegates day-to-day decision making to an executive committee, consisting of the president, secretary, and treasurer. Finally, there is an oversight committee (*comité de vigilancia*) to make sure that everything is done correctly and to watch out for corruption. The typical organization also has administrative staff and advisors.

It seems that a tension between hired staff and peasant leadership more often than not leads to this phenomenon of splitting. The hired staff and advisors often gain unequal power vis-à-vis the members, because of their years of experience in the coffee business and the personal contacts they develop in the market. This knowledge gives them a certain power in organizational decision making. Still, the staff and advisors do not in theory run the organization, as they are subject to the decisions of the general assembly and the political leadership. But a certain, often latent, power struggle is often present, to the point that some advisors may want to leave and do business their own way.

> . . . *hay una contradicción permanente casi natural digamos, entre el asesor y el dirigente campesino. Es una relación como los matrimonios de 50 y 50. Hay una necesidad profesional pero también una disputa, un conflicto, una relación conflictiva. Al principio en las primeras etapas de las organiza-*

94

ciones marchan de maravilla el asesor y el dirigente. El orientador este trae conocimientos, que transfiere de diferentes maneras al dirigente campesino y normalmente los asesores tienen pertenencia institucional. Es muy difícil que cualquier asesor que viene tenga una relación bajo de la estructura de una organización. Es gente de la iglesia o es gente de algún partido político, o es gente de una organización, o es gente colada a un grupo altruista o a una ONG o lo que sea. Entonces él es gente con manejo de relaciones importantes que son benéficas para la organización y benéficas para el dirigente ¿no? se usan mucho las mancuernas ¿no? entonces ahí va el asesor con su dirigente campesino ¿no? que da legitimidad, que vinculan dos mundos, que da sistematización, este, y te da liderazgo, te da conocimientos, te da arraigo, te conforman un liderazgo ahí este . . . importante ¿no? pero al poco tiempo se van. Finalmente cuando tu ya transferiste, y es de los dos lados, como el asesor ya llega a la comunidad, cuando ya tienes libros pus ya no necesitas del dirigente, y cuando el dirigente ya anda con bastante gente, con las fundaciones, con el gobierno, pues para que lo necesita al asesor. Entonces este, se mueven relaciones tormentosas ¿no? pus el asesor, cada quien por su lado ¿no? el asesor empieza pronto a hacer trato, a jalar por su propia cuenta con ciertos grupos, a manejarse en medio de la dirección formal. El líder campesino empieza a prescindir de los consejos del asesor, empieza a tener sus propias líneas de comunicación, digamos pues eso es muy recurrente.

[. . . there is a permanent, almost natural contradiction, you might say, between the advisor and the campesino leader. It's a relationship like those 50:50 marriages where there is both a mutual need but also a dispute, a conflict, a conflictive relationship. In the beginning, in the early stages, everything goes great between the advisor and the leader. The advisor brings knowledge that is transferred in different ways to the campesino leader, but normally the advisor belongs to some type of institution, so they are not likely to accept being under the structure of our organization. It is going to be somebody from the church, or from a political party, someone from some organization, or from some altruistic group or an NGO or whatever. The point is it's someone who manages relationships that are important and beneficial for organization and for the leader. Many times you become buddies, no? "There goes the advisor with his peasant leader." It provides legitimacy, it links two worlds, it help systematize experiences, it gives you leadership, and knowledge, it grounds you, and you build your leadership that way. But little by little things change, on both sides, the knowledge has been transferred, the advisor has access to the community and with all registered in books, then the leader is no longer needed. Now the leader goes around with all kinds of people, with foundations, with the government, so what does he need the advisor for? The relationship turns stormy, no? Sooner or later the advisor starts to make his own deals, to pull certain groups out on his own, to finesse the formal leadership, to become the formal leadership. At the same time the campesino leader can now do without the advice of the advisor, has his own lines of communication, etc. We can say this is very common.]

—Adalberto Santis, campesino leader from the Soconusco

The insertion in the market demands an administrative capacity that makes peasant organizations dependent on professional staff. At the same time, this market is inaccessible for those who are not organized or those who do not know the key people in the solidarity market (Gonzalez, Link, and Moguel 2003, 38). Parra and Moguel (1995, 33) argue that it is impossible for indigenous, campesino coffee producers to take complete control of marketing their coffee, due to issues of language (many do not speak Spanish, much less English) and forms of communication (verbal rather than written, no e-mail, etc.), knowledge of the international market, and the ability to deal with funder and donor organizations. While I did encounter such cases of cultural domination in the field, I also observed that many organizations are developing their negotiation skills in real cross-cultural relationships, in addition to hiring more staff with rural backgrounds.[4]

The Coffee Cooperatives

In the following capsule histories of the six major cooperatives chosen as representative of the overall diversity of coffee organizations in Chiapas, one can appreciate their diverse origins, and also see how each emerged during one or another of the recent cycles of social capital formation.

LÁZARO CÁRDENAS

The Unión de Ejidos Lázaro Cárdenas in the Soconusco region was founded when INMECAFE was the main buyer in this region and the National Confederation of Campesinos (CNC)—affiliated with the PRI—was the main peasant organization. The small coffee producers in the middle of the Soconusco region, normally an area dominated by large producers, were not happy with INMECAFE's practices of preferential buying from the large producers, and the co-op was conceived as an alternative for the small producers. Lázaro Cárdenas was organized in 1979 with the support of Rafael Moreno Martínez, an advisor from the Agrarian Department of the CNC. Eleven ejidos from the municipality of Unión Juárez originally founded the co-op.

The organization was founded to organize coffee producers to obtain financing, to be able to export directly, to improve the marketing of their product, and to lend organizational services to partner organizations. In 1980 it bought four hectares of land with a coffee mill and storage space from Bruno García Robles. The government of PRI governor Juan Sabines Gutiérrez paid 50 percent of the 5 million pesos (US$217,391) required to make this purchase, and the co-op paid the rest. Upon the purchase of this new infrastructure, located in the city of Cacahoatán, ejidos from the municipalities of Cacahoatán, Tuxtla Chico, and Tapachula joined the eleven ejidos that had formed Lázaro Cárdenas, bringing its membership to thirty-two ejidos.

The cooperative became a player in the export market; they delivered coffee to INMECAFE as well as exporting on their own. When IN-MECAFE disappeared, the co-op obtained an export permit and went on to become one of the biggest exporters in the region.

Currently there are twenty-four ejidos with a total of twelve hundred members in the Lázaro Cárdenas cooperative. The co-op changes representatives every three years and holds monthly meetings attended by two delegates from each ejido. None of the representative posts receives any kind of remuneration; all are considered service positions. The co-op itself is a member of both the Unión Estatal de Productores de Café and the Unión Nacional de Productores de Café, both of which belong to the CNC.

The co-op has worked with credit from Bancrisa and from the Fondo Nacional de Apajoa Empresas de Solidaridad (FONAES). The credit is used for cultivation and harvesting. Members buy chemical fertilizer and pay their workers with credit, which is deducted when they deliver their harvest to the co-op. Lázaro Cárdenas members have the right to process their coffee in the coffee mill and either sell it to the co-op or sell it else-where. The ten technicians who work for the co-op are paid with funds from a development program.

Despite its successes, the co-op has also suffered setbacks. With the general fall of coffee prices and the disappearance of INMECAFE in 1989, Lázaro Cárdenas was already in shaky financial shape. When two buyers did not pay the co-op for eighteen hundred sacks of coffee, the co-op found itself unable to pay its members. Later, with new leaders and the support of the Mexican government's National Indigenous Institute (INI), the co-op was able to pay back this debt during the years of good prices. Then, in order to upgrade their machinery, the co-op began to seek op-portunities to earn money wherever possible.

In 1992 a new board of directors was elected from a reformist section of the CNC. The new directors focused on production and decided to open the mill and offer processing and other services to other co-ops or anyone else willing to pay. This open policy generated a tense relation-ship with state authorities, and many members left the co-op when oppo-sition parties suggested that it not pay back the credit that programs like the National Solidarity Program (PRONASOL) had provided for its members.

MAJOMUT

In the highlands of Chiapas many UEPCs were formed. In 1980 and 1981 a number of local groups of coffee farmers came together to request that all project resources be given directly to the communities. During these meetings it was suggested that a storage shed be built to store members' produce, to then be sold at a better price on the local and regional markets. The building of this storage area was also a response to INMECAFE's faulty coffee collection practices. Apparently, INMECAFE had a secret agreement with local middlemen in the town of Panthelhó under which INMECAFE would mysteriously be closed on certain days so the middlemen could buy all the coffee at a lower price than would have been offered to the producers. The following day the middlemen would sell the coffee to INMECAFE for a better price. The new storage shed would provide a place for producers from distant towns to leave their coffee cargo until the INMECAFE store reopened.

Eighteen communities from two municipalities were selected to begin the negotiations with regional representatives from PIDER, and in 1982 they agreed to build the storage shed in the town of Majomut, in the municipality of Polho (Mayan Tzotzil for "place where the birds fight"). A recognized legal incorporation was needed to receive the facility, so the Agrarian Reform and Indigenous Affairs Secretaries approved the creation of the Unión de Ejidos and the Comunidades de Cafeticultores del Beneficio Majomut S. de R.I. (Majomut 1996).

The main objectives of the organization were the following:

- to pursue the cultivation, industrialization, and commercialization of coffee and its derivatives on an international and national level,
- to build, acquire, and establish industries and services, use renewable and nonrenewable resources, distribute and commercialize the products, manage credits, and in general engage in all classes of industries, services, and rural activities,
- to promote the economic improvement and material progress of the members, as well as the capitalization of the ejido and the community,
- to carry out all economic or material transactions to improve the collective organization of work, as well as to increase crop productivity, and use of available resources.

Today, three agrarian communities and two ejidos legally form the Unión de Ejidos y Comunidades Majomut.[5] The executive committee is in charge of marketing, and the oversight committee is in charge of collecting the harvest and looking after the fixed assets of the organization (machinery, trucks, coffee mill, storage facilities). Usually both committees have three-year terms, although circumstances can vary. For example, in the uncertainty in the wake of the 1997 Acteal massacre, the general assembly decided to extend their terms of office for another term. The members are represented by two delegates from each of the thirty-two towns that participate and conduct monthly meetings and annual assemblies.

Majomut sold its first shipment under a contract from La Selva (see below). The idea was that they would cooperate and learn from La Selva's experience until it could become self-sufficient and create its own roster of clients, which they were soon able to do. Over the years the cooperative has managed to survive despite setbacks, as when coffee prices fell in the late 1980s, or when two buyers declared bankruptcy in 1988, or when the co-op's president was falsely accused of embezzlement.

In 1992 Unión Majomut began to seek alternatives to the crisis brought on by the disappearance of the ICA and INMECAFE, including the promotion of conversion to organic technology on the mostly communal lands of the Majomut members in 1993. The transition to organic took less time than it did for other organizations, because the generalized lack of economic resources among the Majomut membership had prevented most of the producers from applying agrochemicals for many years (Perezgrovas et al. 1997).

This organization has a professional staff and advisors, as well as grant support from the Rockefeller and the Inter-American Foundations. Majomut has, in recent years, emphasized diversification, expanding its focus beyond coffee production to self-sufficiency through the planting of food crops, a family garden, reforestation, housing construction, transportation, and nutrition programs. In proportional terms, Majomut members have dedicated more of their land to the cultivation of maize than have members of other coffee organizations. Furthermore, 50 percent of the production of fifteen hundred Majomut members is currently completely organic, 30 percent is being converted to organic, and 20 percent uses traditional/natural technology (interview with Majomut Representatives, March 2002).

There is a range of political affiliations within the membership of Majomut, and its relationship with the autonomous Zapatista authorities is cordial. All ejido members can be part of Majomut without regard to political affiliation, as economic interests are put ahead of politics. This priority continued even after the formation of the Zapatista autonomous municipality of Polho in 1996 and the consequent division of municipal authorities. In the late 1990s 65 percent of Majomut's member communities were Zapatista bases.

Because the organization is relatively strong and because it was helped by other organizations early on, Majomut has a general policy of helping other, smaller and newer, organizations to enter the market. Its members have also learned that exporting in collaboration with other organizations lowers export costs (interview with Majomut representatives, March 2002).

ISMAM

The Indígenas de la Sierra Madre de Motozintla "San Isidro Labrador" cooperative (ISMAM) was founded in 1987 to provide an alternative marketing channel to middlemen and became the most successful organic coffee cooperative in Chiapas in the 1990s. The Catholic Church played an important role in its formation, and the support of the government and international NGOs has been critical to its development and growth. The Catholic dioceses of Tapachula are organized in *foranias*,[6] or regions. The forania of the sierra has five commissions, which address health, women, youth, human rights and cooperatives, the latter of which is in charge of organizing agricultural cooperatives. The cooperative commission promotes alternative agriculture and aquaculture, develops new models of commercialization and production, and promotes savings plans and credit programs.

Father Jorge Aguilar Reyna, coordinator of the Sierra Forania at that time, was crucial in the formation of ISMAM. Towards the end of 1985 the Sierra Forania organized a coffee producers meeting in which a subgroup was named to look into the best way to start a production and marketing organization. The group, accompanied by Father Reyna, went to Oaxaca and established contact with UCIRI, a union that was already producing certified organic coffee. It began experimenting with compost, and had a general meeting in mid-1986 to elect representatives and leaders by region. It defined itself as an organization "of service not business," and decided to use only biological agriculture methods to produce a better quality product and to protect the environment and its members' health. ISMAM was one of the organizations that promoted the Organized Communal Labor (TCO) program, in which producers organized themselves in groups to exchange labor. This was a revitalization of the collective work known as *tequio*[7] in Mexico. TCO implied extra work, little credit, a lot of meetings, and heavy service requirements. Many farmers were unwilling to accept this burden and, of the 250 producers that originally met, only 99 decided to continue in ISMAM.

ISMAM, as well as the other coffee organizations, was spurred on by the collapse of the ICO agreement and the 30 percent drop in coffee prices over the following three days. Coffee producers were thus forced to look for alternative ways to sell their coffee. At the same time the market for organic products in Europe had begun to grow. The ISMAM consultants soon learned of this growth potential in the organic market from the international meetings of IFOAM that they attended.

The initial development of ISMAM was supported by a grant from the importing organization SOS Werdeldhandel in the Netherlands.[8] In these initial efforts, UCIRI supported ISMAM by selling part of ISMAM's harvest. With the help of the Max Havelaar Fair Trade Association of Denmark to commercialize its product, ISMAM soon overcame its initial membership loss and by 1990 had 490 members (Sánchez 1990). IFOAM also contributed, with training in organic practices and principles. The Mexican nonprofit dedicated to supporting indigenous communities, Maderas del Pueblo, provided training in composting, erosion control, and the intercropping of other crops with coffee. Today, ISMAM coffee is certified as organic by the German-based certification agency Naturland.

The fundamental goal of the cooperative is to concentrate the production of its many members in order to facilitate direct export, eliminate intermediaries, and recover greater value added for their product. ISMAM obtained one of the largest and most modern coffee mills in Chiapas in 1992 when the government sold it to them on credit as a part of the privatization of INMECAFE.

ISMAM sales rivaled the government largesse. In 1990 sales were estimated at US$900,000. They rose to $1.5 million in 1991, to $2.4 million in 1992, to $3.2 million in 1993, and in 1994 they totaled $4.8 million. By 1995 they had 1,529 members, whose average annual income was $1,850, an exceptionally high income in indigenous, rural Chiapas (Meda 1995).

ISMAM's structure reflects a commitment to democratic principles. Its members attempt to reach a consensus in decision making, but they also vote on a measure when there is no consensus. The cooperative was organized to give local members some degree of autonomy, so each community has two representatives that attend general assemblies. The cooperative is organized into six committees: executive, controller, finance, education, technical assistance, and other issues (Nigh 1992).

The collective decision to adopt organic farming had profound impacts on ISMAM members. Organic farming requires strict internal control of all phases of production in order to maintain certification. ISMAM established a system in which each bag could be traced to its origin. Its own agronomist (who is independent from the government extension agent) makes monthly visits to the members' farms and takes notes about organic fertilizing, the condition of the groves, and other agricultural practices, which are archived in a computer in the co-op's central office (Nigh 1997). This process helped ISMAM perfect its levels of internal organization. Currently all ISMAM producers are 100 percent organic.

LA SELVA

Extensive colonization had already taken place in the Lacandón jungle by 1972, when President Luis Echeverría (1970–76) decreed a land grant of six hundred thousand hectares of jungle to sixty Lacandón families. The other inhabitants of the jungle, colonists who had arrived in previous years, fought for their right to land. Many groups were relocated and granted ejidos, or they were given the option to purchase land elsewhere. Many others remained in militant struggle, which resulted in them being severely repressed. Local organizations of peasants with land decided to promote productive projects rather than join the others and risk repression over land issues (Pérez Arce 1991, cited in Wohlgemuth 1996).

The Unión de Uniones (UUE), formed during the 1970s social capital cycle, split in 1989. There were too many members spread out over too large a geographical area. Communication and coordination became very difficult, and, as a result, decision making became too centralized. The rupture of the UUE was not particularly contentious; rather a group of producers and advisors began to focus on coffee and look out for better prices and other options.

Later that year they formed the Unión de Ejidos de la Selva. The idea was to focus on the production and commercialization of coffee using the combined experience of the group. They were Tojolobal and Tzeltal Mayan Indians with land, from the municipalities of Independencia, Margaritas, Palenque, and Trinitaria, and later, from the highland municipality of Tenejapa. La Selva has had a good deal of turnover, as member communities have come and gone over the years. Several groups left in 1994 to join the Zapatistas. Currently, there are thirteen hundred members living in eight municipalities: Bella Vista, Chicomuselo, Independencia, Margaritas, Siltepec, Trinitaria, Ocosingo, and Oxchuc.

Their first coffee was shipped through UCIRI, at a time when that organization had more demand than production and was willing to help commercialize coffee from new coffee organizations. La Selva has been a leader in organizing various networks and participates in many of them. The influence of the Catholic teachings was strong on La Selva members; in particular, its "Pastoral de la Tierra," which promoted the idea of Mother Earth, helped La Selva members switch their production to organic methods. UCIRI also suggested that they should produce organically.

The conversion to organic began in 1991 and was relatively easy and fast because its members had rarely used agrochemicals. La Selva quickly obtained certification from OCIA (the U.S.-based certification agency) and Naturland (German based). They marketed their coffee with the Max Havelaar label in Europe and under the Aztec Harvest label through the CNOC office in the United States.

In 1990, La Selva, together with three other cooperatives,[9] opened a commercial processor known as the Coffee Producers' Union of the Southern Border (UNCAFESUR), with offices in the city of Comitán. They bought a coffee mill in Comitán with funds from the INI and the National Solidarity Program (PRONASOL). The co-op has a technical team of professional advisors on organic farming and has begun to train a group of campesino technicians to replace the professional ones.

When the Zapatista uprising began in 1994, many members of La Selva abandoned their homes to seek refuge in the town of Las Margaritas. It was there that the Church, humanitarian groups, and governmental programs helped them survive for more than a year. La Selva provided support for these members but could not harvest their coffee and, as a result, it suffered a crisis. Although it was a difficult time, good coffee prices in subsequent years helped members recover their losses.

La Selva has initiated several projects for its members, such as the construction of schools, houses, drying patios, and health clinics, with funds obtained through the sales they have made under fair trade conditions, and with some grants. More recently, however, the co-op has set aside such community projects and now focuses only on coffee.

La Selva opened its first coffee shop in San Cristóbal in the mid-1990s and later opened another in Mexico City. The idea was to focus on and expand the national market for coffee so as not to depend solely on the international market. Currently, the co-op has a franchise program in which owners of coffee shops in Mexico and abroad adopt the La Selva logo and store style and sell only La Selva coffee.

Tzotzilotic Tzobolotic

The Sociedad Cooperativa Tzotzilotic Tzobolotic (Mayan Tzotzil people united) was formed when fifteen communities quit the Unión Pajal Yakaltik, which had been created during the 1970s. The Pajal was an organization supported by advisors from Línea Proletaria that in the early seventies tried to organize a coalition between farmworkers and factory workers. In those years, the main concern of the members was to obtain land. This quest took on various forms, and some chose to engage in land occupations, while others purchased their plots.

Over time the tactics of Pajal Yakaltik shifted according to what was happening on a national level, especially with the tendencies toward *cambio de terreno* (appropriation of the production process). It took some time for the members to understand why the focus had switched from land invasions to production. This was the beginning of schisms among the member communities in which some stuck with confrontational tactics of land occupation, while others moved toward formation of credit unions and negotiations to buy land.

When the fifteen communities left Pajal Yakaltic, they started a process of involvement in workshops, courses, and discussions for the community members and advisors. Tzotzilotic Tzobolotic attained legal status in 1992, with six hundred members from the municipality of El Bosque in the highlands of Chiapas. Their structure is democratic with delegates from each town. They have an annual general assembly in December or January where all the main decisions are made. Three leaders are elected in the general assembly and their posts last from five to seven years. Many members belong to the Labor Party and are very active in local politics. This makes this cooperative different from the others in the sense that the leaders are actively involved in politics, and they haven't had the time to try to tap into the fair trade market nor the organic production process.

Tzotzilotic sells principally to the conventional coffee market, though it has recently begun conversion to organic production in hopes of getting a better price and because most small-farm export production in Chiapas is now organic. As a member of the CNOC, the co-op has exported to Germany and the United States.

Tzotzilotic has obtained loans from private banks to finance purchasing the harvest of its members. When prices are low, the co-op is able to get early credit and it can thus buy large quantities of coffee and move it quickly. It also pays higher prices to its members than those offered by middlemen (*coyotes*). When coffee prices rise during the harvest season, they complicate things for the coffee co-ops. A given amount of credit now buys less coffee, thus making it hard for the co-op to meet contracted quantities. To pay the higher price to its members, the co-op pays an advance and the balance is paid when the coffee is sold. As a result, some of the co-op's members sell to middlemen who pay in cash. When coffee prices are high all coffee co-ops find it difficult to beat out the middlemen.

The Tzotzilotic co-op functions as the de facto regulator of prices in the western highlands. When the prices are set for its members, the middlemen cannot go any lower, and this situation effects other cooperatives throughout the region.

The co-op sells some ground and roasted coffee to the national market, mainly to customers in Zamora, Michoacán, Palenque, and San Cristóbal. Tzotzilotic holds fair trade certification, but it hasn't been able to find a buyer for any coffee under fair trade labels yet. However, it has been able to sell honey from its apiculture project through the Max Havelaar ATO. The co-op has a group of farmer-technicians that give technical advice to the other members. It used to have a professional agronomist in charge of the technical area, but now it relies on campesinos as technical promoters that live in the community and can visit the farms more frequently.

In 1994 the co-op's members were divided by the Zapatista rebellion. Almost half left the organization to form Zapatista bases. The initial division was political, and in some cases members of the same families went in different directions, although both groups shared the same space in the municipality of El Bosque. The Zapatista group later went on to form the MutVitz co-op.

The organization of coffee producers called MutVitz (Tzotzil for Bird Mountain) was formed after the 1994 Zapatista uprising. Although the previous organization (Partido del Trabajo) was also on the left, its leadership found the hard and clear-cut Zapatista line—"We will have nothing to do with the state"—very difficult to accept. The Zapatistas, with their principle of autonomy, are completely divorced from the government, and MutVitz is allied with them and with international Zapatista solidarity groups. Although the split in the original co-op was not particularly confrontational, members of the former organization criticize the Zapatistas for using armed struggle and for "wasting" work time in demonstrations and marches.

The one thousand, mostly Tzotzil, members of MutVitz come from Zapatista autonomous communities in the highlands of Chiapas, spread across the current municipalities of Bochil, El Bosque, Chenalhó, Jitotol, Larrainzar, and Simojovel. It has some fifty peasant "promoters," who teach organic farming practices to the members, similar to the formula now employed by many campesino organizations. MutVitz's members say that the switch from professional technicians to campesino promoters has resulted in better follow-up and continuity and ensures that the promoters know the local area well, rather than technicians who they say have book knowledge but no experience to back it up.

Earlier, the Zapatista coffee farmers in this area had worked for a number of years without a formal organization, selling their coffee to local middlemen. In 1997, during a period of good prices, as part of their search for alternatives to the middlemen, and responding to interest expressed by international Zapatista solidarity buyers, they organized themselves formally. They took on the name of the principal mountain in their region and obtained legal registry in 1998 as a *sociedad de solidaridad social* (SSS, or "Triple S"), but they are organized as a commercial cooperative. Also in 1998 they obtained their official coffee export permit.

The co-op's first foreign buyers came through solidarity channels from the United States and Italy. After getting all their legal paperwork in order, it started looking into the fair trade market. In 1999 MutVitz sent its first transshipment container of coffee to the United States. That sale was a big success with the members, as middlemen were paying everybody else in the region US$1.24/kg (or 12 pesos/kg), while members of MutVitz received $1.86/kg (18 pesos/kg). Their fruitful entry into the export market facilitated the consolidation of the organization, and soon a growing number of farmers were interested in joining.

MutVitz has followed the same path to organic conversion that other coffee organizations in the highlands have pursued. The members that decide to transition to organic first experiment on small plots and then apply the technology to the rest of their grove. Today, with coffee prices at a low point, most MutVitz members have completed the conversion to organic.

They sell through both the solidarity and the organic markets, often at better prices than those received by other coffee organizations in the area and also better than Zapatista coffee producers that remain unorganized.

MutVitz has an agroecological program whose objectives are to increase the knowledge members have of alternative technology, improve the ability of the members to sell coffee at fair prices, improve the basic infrastructure of member families, and improve the dry-processing and transport infrastructure. The overarching goal is to improve the overall economic and social well-being of the members.

Since the members of MutVitz are Zapatistas, they have been subjected to state and military repression. Their region has had several military checkpoints since 1995, and all who pass them are subject to registry. At the five checkpoints between the town of San Juan de la Libertad, where the MutVitz warehouse is located, and San Cristóbal de las Casas, where most of their business transactions take place, members are stopped, must show papers, are often interrogated, and generally feel harassed. They felt that they are forced by the authorities to waste a lot of valuable time (president of MutVitz, interview by Cloud Forest Initiative, March 2000). The checkpoints were dismantled in 2001 when President Vicente Fox made a pledge to the Zapatistas to remove certain military bases in order to restart peace negotiations. However, the base at the main crossroads of the MutVitz region is still there, and paramilitary forces remain abundant in the western highlands. In 2000, MutVitz reported the killings of several of its members by paramilitaries.

In 1999 MutVitz sold its first two containers of coffee with fair trade certification, and has found this to be advantageous. The co-op sells through the Cloud Forest Initiative, the Human Bean Company, and other channels, and is doing quite well for such a young co-op. As its access to resources grows, MutVitz is planning to offer credit to its members.

Other Organizations

Some coffee-producing families in Chiapas have not affiliated themselves with any organization. Others have joined together to form very small, local organizations. Many of these minuscule cooperatives exist all over Chiapas. In general, they have had far less success than the larger organizations described above, demonstrating how the ability to "scale up" is critical in the coffee-producing social sector. Without having achieved regional scope, these organizations have not been able to successfully tap into the international market.

One such smaller organization, COTZEPEC, in Tenejapa, was created with support from the INI and INMECAFE. During the economic crisis at the beginning of the 1980s, the support, advice, and resources channeled through the INI office in Tenejapa promoted the organizing of campesinos and the search for economic alternatives (Parra and Moguel 1996).

The indigenous farmers in COTZEPEC faced one obstacle after another, starting with problems registering themselves as a legal entity. Once they adopted legal forms of association, decision making about the production process shifted from the family to an institutional framework for planning production. Their first legal representatives were young, educated Tenejapans who soon acquired the corrupt practices of INMECAFE and were later expelled from the community for mismanagement. Once INMECAFE was out of the picture, the INI stepped in again and changed the leadership formula to community committees (*comités comunitarios*). However, then-governor Patrocinio Gonzales Garrido, a well-known reactionary, was opposed to the progressive position of the INI officials and they were expelled from Chiapas. Soon thereafter COTZEPEC had a serious problem of fraud in the sale of their 1995 harvest. To date the organization has not recovered from these multiple setbacks.

Chapter 8

The Economic Benefits of Organic Farming

THE DIFFERENT TECHNOLOGICAL approaches used in coffee farming—natural, chemical, transitional, and organic—are in fact different approaches to investment (or in some cases disinvestment) in land, which, along with resources like water and biodiversity, is part of natural capital. In seeking to know what the benefits—or costs—of these strategies are for the families that implement them, it is important to note that technological strategies tend to vary from organization to organization. We can thus expect that the benefits and costs will vary as well, creating a linkage between social capital and natural capital that has already been explored theoretically in chapter 6.

TO CHARACTERIZE THE approach to cultivation used by the coffee producers surveyed in this study, visits to the coffee groves were made to visually obtain the information from the farm. The visits were conducted together with the farmer. While walking across the grove, farmers were asked about their agronomic practices (terraces, weeding, pruning, fertilization, etc.), which were also visually confirmed in their parcel. Information on the coffee varieties planted, secondary crops, biodiversity, and so on, was also obtained. In these visits measurements were taken to make estimates of shade cover and diversity, soil erosion, leaf litter cover, and humus layer.

Shade coverage was visually estimated and ranked on a visual index ranging from No Shade (no trees, or almost no trees present) to 100 Percent Shade (no direct sunlight penetration). The general health and vigor of the coffee plants was noted by the color of foliage, the presence of pest damage, and the general appearance of the plants. Planting density was calculated from eight measurements of the distance between coffee plants made at eight random points in different sections of each grove. The farmers surveyed were classified as organic, natural, in transition to organic, or conventional based on the data collected during the visit to the coffee grove.

A prime indicator of the economic benefits a given technology offers for farm families is yield. In general we expect that as smallholders intensify production by investing more labor, capital, and inputs in it, yield goes up. One caveat, however: yield—which is usually expressed as the quantity of a single product harvested per unit area—tends to underestimate the true productivity of smaller farmers (Rosset 1999). This is because small farmers often produce many different crops, and even animals, yet yield refers to only one of these products. Furthermore, intensification itself may occur by adding additional components to the mix (e.g., intercropping or, in the case of coffee, adding shade trees that produce other useful products) rather than by increasing the intensity of production of single crop. Nevertheless, the productivity of coffee *is* of prime importance to farmers for whom it is their major income source, and there exists a common tendency to intensify the production of coffee itself, in order to boost this income source, especially in years with good prices.

How Technologies and Geographies Affect Yield

The expectation one has in terms of technology and yield depends on one's preconceived notions. Those who believe that organic farming constitutes a return to premodernity expect that organic farmers will have much lower yields than chemical farmers. These skeptics tend to see organic farming as the antithesis of intensification and chemically assisted farming as its realization. Proponents of organic farming, on the other hand, feel that both chemical and organic methods can intensify production.

In the conventional view, on organic farms—and those in transition to organic—yields would be expected to differ little from those in natural (nonintensive) production, while on farms in chemical production, yields would be much higher than any of the other methods. This pattern might be represented as

Chemical > Organic = Transitional = Natural

(chemical is greater than organic, transitional, and natural—all of which are the roughly the same as each other).

An organic farming advocate, on the other hand, would expect chemical and organic yields to be expected to be similar, with both being significantly higher than for farms in natural production. Transitional would be somewhere in between:

Chemical = Organic > Transitional > Natural.

A simple analysis of the 110 families from whom yield estimates were obtained,[1] revealed a pattern that falls somewhere in between the two stereotypical expectations described above:

Chemical > Organic > Transitional > Natural

(see table 8.1). However, the data are not quite statistically significant, making it difficult to conclude that the pattern is real and not simply due to chance.

It is likely that the effect of using all four technologies in different regions—with altitudes, soils, and weather patterns radically different in their suitability for coffee—statistically confounds the effect of technology, and that is why the results are not statistically significant. In fact, when

TABLE 8.1
Coffee yield by technology (qq/ha)

Factors	Mean	± Standard error
Natural	7.54	± 1.68
Transitional	8.44	± 1.02
Organic	10.26	± 0.78
Chemical	11.40	± 1.31

Notes: The standard measure of coffee yield is in quintales of green coffee beans per hectare (qq/ha). One quintal (hundredweight) equals 100 pounds, or 45.4 kg. Differences are not significant (p = .1544; N = 110).

analyzed alone, the geographic region in which a farm is located does very much affect yields. A simple analysis of how yield varies by region revealed significant differences expressed by the pattern

Soconusco > sierra > western highlands ≥
north > eastern highlands > jungle

(see table 8.2). That ranking seems to follow a ranking of soil quality in which the Soconusco has the best coffee soils and the jungle the worst. The Soconusco was the original area where coffee was introduced into Chiapas and the jungle the last with the lowest altitudes. Soconusco is also the more specialized area in coffee production with sampled families dedicating less than 5 percent of land to other crops and the majority of producers using chemical inputs.

Given the significant effect of region on average yield, it is likely that the effect of technology in the earlier analysis was, indeed, confounded by the regions where the technologies were employed. In order to separate confounding effects (which could include a confounding effect of technology on region as well), it was necessary to use an analysis that relies on multiple variables.[2]

The analysis for regions and technologies revealed significant effects on yields of both regions and technologies, and one significant interaction between them (a statistical interaction would be where the effect of a particular technology is different in different regions). Three regions had distinct effects in the statistical model (jungle, Soconusco, sierra), as did all

TABLE 8.2
Coffee yield by region (qq/ha)

Factors	Mean	± Standard error
Jungle	5.68	1.43
North	9.86	1.30
Highland West	9.68	0.98
Highland East	8.86	1.07
Soconusco	13.07	1.62
Sierra	12.40	1.49

Note: Differences are significant ($p < .01$; $N = 110$).

the technologies, plus a very positive interaction between organic technology and the sierra region. Perhaps this interaction is due to the effect of the
ISMAM cooperative, which is dominant in the sierra. Since ISMAM has
been producing organic coffee for many more years than any other organization, its members may be more skilled at coffee production practices. At
the same time, the most motivated, innovative, and convinced campesino
promoter I encountered was from ISMAM in this region. Here his con-
tinuous work with groups of producers and showing by example were
motivators for the rest.

A simple statistical model relating yield to regions and technologies
was generated:

$$Y = 8.6 - 3.8(J) + 2.9(So) - 1.3(Si) + 0.3(T) +$$
$$1.3(Or) + 1.8(C) + 6.0(Or \times Si)$$

where: Y = yield (qq/ha), J = jungle, So = Soconusco, Si = sierra, T = transitional, Or = organic, C = chemical, and the variables for regions and
technologies are what statisticians call dummy variables, each of which
can take on the value of either 0 or 1 (that is, they are either present or
not—either "on" or "off"). This model allows us to estimate yields for
each technology, corrected for the effect of various regions. These corrected yields are presented in table 8.3 and are shown graphically (in comparison to the raw, uncorrected yields) in figure 8.1.

The differences among the raw yields of the various regions studied, although they appear larger than the differences in the corrected yields,
were not statistically significant. The differences among the corrected
yields, however, were statistically significant. The neat step-by-step pattern

TABLE 8.3
Coffee yield by technology, corrected for effect of region (qq/ha)

Technology	Mean yield	± Standard error
Natural	8.57	1.65
Transitional	8.87	1.92
Organic	9.85	1.80
Chemical	10.32	3.44

Note: Differences are significant ($p < .05$; $N = 110$).

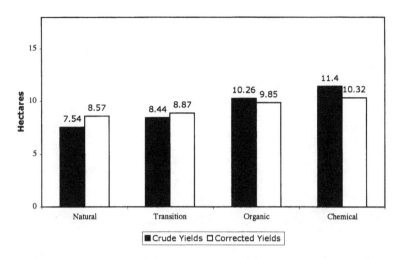

Figure 8.1. Raw yields by technology. *Note:* Yields corrected for effect of region.

of increases in the raw yields along the presumptive continuum of intensification, from natural to transitional through organic and then chemical, has been replaced by a pattern in which a slight increase between natural and transitional is followed by a jump to organic and chemical. (Figure 8.2 shows the average yield increase over natural technology obtained with transitional, organic, and chemical technologies.)

While this finding still falls somewhere between the expectations of advocates and skeptics of organic farming, it is much closer to the expectation of the former

Chemical = Organic > Transitional > Natural

than to the latter, who expected

Chemical > Organic = Transitional = Natural.

In other words, it lends support to the hypothesis that investment in natural capital via organic farming practices is indeed a viable alternative route to the intensification of coffee production through chemical inputs. And it puts paid to the conventional wisdom that organic farming is the low-yield "opposite" of intensification.

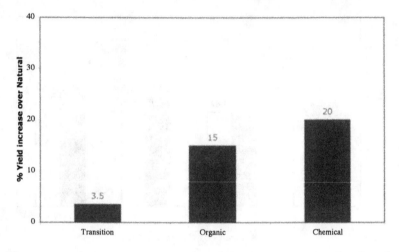

Figure 8.2. Average yield increase by technology (percent). *Note:* Data based on mean yields corrected for effect of region.

Returning to the correction of yields for the effect of region, it indeed turns out that, for the raw data, region confounded the effect of technology on yield, and vice versa. In order to view the full picture, the statistical model was used to generate corrected yields for each combination of region and technology (see table 8.4).

When these corrected yields are plotted out (figure 8.3), they show a uniform pattern for both technology and region, with the exception of organic coffee in the sierra region. The sierra region is where ISMAM dominates organic coffee production, and clearly it is doing something right—organic technology actually outproduces chemical technology in this region. While this may speak, on the one hand, to ISMAM's efficient organization and probably to agroclimatological conditions in the sierra and their aptness for organic production as well, it also indicates the potential that organic production offers as an intensification strategy, a potential that is as yet not fully exploited in most regions.[3]

Income and Technology

When speaking of a cash, rather than a subsistence, crop, increases in yield mean little if not translated into income gains. Gross income from coffee

TABLE 8.4
Corrected mean yields for each combination of region and technology (qq/ha)

Region	Technology	Corrected yield
Jungle	natural	4.8
	transitional	5.1
	organic	6.1
	chemical	6.6
Soconusco	natural	11.5
	transitional	11.8
	organic	12.8
	chemical	13.3
Sierra	natural	7.3
	transitional	7.6
	organic	14.6
	chemical	9.1
HE, HW, north	natural	8.6
	transitional	8.9
	organic	9.9
	chemical	10.4

Note: Differences are significant ($p < .05$, $N = 100$).

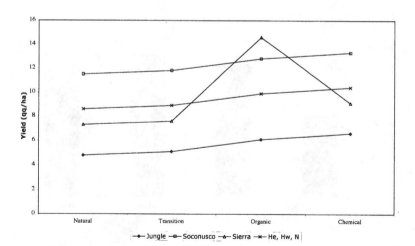

Figure 8.3. Corrected mean yields by region, technology

depends on a combination of yield, area harvested, quality, and price; and the latter is mitigated by a variety of factors, such as sale to the organization versus sale to an intermediary, or coyote. Figure 8.4 presents gross annual income per hectare of coffee.[4] Here there is a substantial step from natural (5,523 pesos/ha) to transitional (8,867 pesos/ha), and from transitional to organic (9,560 pesos/ha), which is virtually the same as chemical (9,732 pesos/ha), although the differences are not quite statistically significant.

This lends further support to organic farming as a viable alternative to chemicals as a means of intensification of production. Organic farming is especially appropriate for cash-poor families in an environment like that common in Chiapas, in which underemployment is high and the opportunity cost for extra family labor low. The investment in organic technology is "cash cheap" and labor intensive, the opposite of chemical technology (Heinegg and Ferroggiaro 1996). A technology that is more labor intensive can be an advantage or a disadvantage depending on alternative employment opportunities, or lack thereof. In many regions of Chiapas that lack good communication, such as the jungle area, there are few opportunities to turn underused family labor into income. Families in such regions have little cash to invest in their coffee production, but they do have family

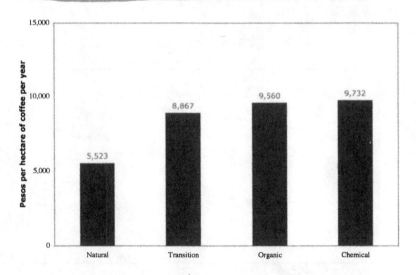

$p = .17$

Figure 8.4. Average gross annual income from coffee per hectare in Chiapas

labor available. Given the alternatives of a labor-saving, capital-intensive route to intensification (chemical production) versus a capital-saving, labor-intensive route (organic) the advantages of the latter are clear. Thus, organic farming may confer an advantage to families with the ability to "self-exploit" their own labor (Chayanov 1986; see Ellis 1988 for another discussion of the peasant economy and self-exploitation). Migration is another alternative for excess family labor—thus it may be fairer to say that, in the words of an indigenous agroecology promoter from the Roberto Barrios community in the non-coffee-producing part of the jungle region, "organic farming is the alternative to migration if we want to hold our communities together" (interview, April 2002).

Furthermore, the differences in income between organic and chemical production are much smaller even than the differences in yield, due to the price premium paid for organic coffee. From 1994 to 1998, for which this data was collected, international coffee prices were much higher than they have been since. When coffee prices are high, the price differential between organic and conventional coffee is relatively slight compared to low-price years, when the premium for organic is much greater. Thus, it would be reasonable to assume that if similar data were available for subsequent low-price years, it would show that organic production actually outperforms chemical in terms of gross income.

Conversion to organic production is thus not only a worthy investment in natural capital, but it pays off in economic terms because organic certification allows the positive benefits for the environment to be "internalized" and thus realized in monetary terms, in the form of price premiums. However, this internalization of benefits requires the prior formation of significant social capital, without which certification and price premiums are impossible to achieve.

Chapter 9

The Ecological Benefits of Organic Farming

IF WE ARE interested in organic farming as an approach that may contribute more to sustainable development, then we must go beyond economic benefits and look at ecological ones as well. Farming of any kind has impacts on ecological variables like biodiversity and the quality of the soil (erosion and soil fertility). Not only are these aspects of the environment important from a purely ecological or conservationist point of view, they may also have significant implications for the sustainability of production into the future. If all of a region's topsoil is eroded away, for example, then future production will become impossible. Thus the ecological variables of today often become *economic* variables in the future. In this sense, when farmers make investments in their natural capital (e.g., their soil or their biodiversity), these investments bring not only a short-term ecological return, but also very likely an economic return over the medium term (see chapter 4 for a theoretical discussion of these issues).

The Ecological Indicators Measured in This Study

The use of a reduced number of ecological variables as indicators of *ecological sustainability* has been well developed in the agro-ecological literature (see for example Altieri 1995; Masera, Astier, and Puentes 1995).

Several ecological measurements in each coffee grove were performed to use as indicators in order to gauge environmental impact. The three most significant areas in which typical agricultural practices in Chiapas are thought to be *un*sustainable are loss of natural soil fertility/quality due to declining organic matter content in the soil (Deinlein 1993; Parra 1989); soil erosion due to the propensity to cultivate steep slopes (Burbach and Rosset 1994; Seggern 1993); and loss of biodiversity due to the replacement of diverse traditional systems with monocultures (Howard 1995; Perfecto, Rice, Greenberg, and Van der Voort 1996).

Soil erosion, coverage by leaf litter/humus, and shade biodiversity were selected as indicators of ecological sustainability. Soil erosion[1] is probably the most direct, short-to-medium-term threat to the sustainability of production, as erosion implies the direct loss of natural capital. On the other hand, the soil is somewhat protected from the direct action of water and wind when it is completely covered by a layer of leaf litter.[2] And the depth of the layer of leaf litter and humus indicates the amount of organic matter that will contribute to future soil fertility via decomposition. Finally, shade biodiversity[3] is a strong determining factor for most other elements of biodiversity, which in turn depend directly or indirectly on vegetational resources; such elements range from birds, mammals, insects and other organisms in the above-ground environment, to the soil biota, which is critical to soil fertility and is most likely enhanced by a greater diversity of leaf litter.

SHADE DIVERSITY AND YIELD

Surprisingly, the ecological data collected on the farms of the participants in this study suggest that shade diversity has a significant effect on coffee yields. In fact, several other studies (Soto 2001) have reached the same conclusions. By statistically fitting a curve to the coffee yield versus the number of species of shade trees on each farm (figure 9.1), a statistically significant positive relationship was found. Perhaps diversity improves yield by promoting decomposition and soil biology, or by enhancing natural controls on pests and diseases of the coffee trees. Whatever the underlying mechanisms, however, planting a greater diversity of shade species in their coffee groves is a useful way for farmers to invest in their natural capital.

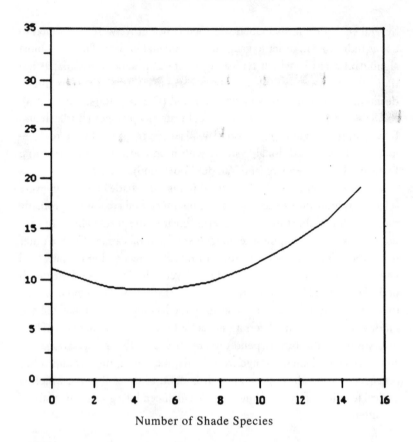

Figure 9.1. Yield by number of shade species. *Note:* This is a curve statistically fitted to the data. The equation is yield $= 11.1 - 0.9n + 0.1n^2$, where n is the number of shade species present in the coffee grove ($R^2 = 0.09$, $p = .03$).

SHADE ACROSS VARIOUS FARMING TECHNOLOGIES

Table 9.1 presents the number of shade species that farmers using different technologies have in their coffee groves. The far lower shade diversity found among chemical growers is interesting—but not surprising. Over 90 percent of chemical growers had fewer than five species of shade trees, while 60 percent of organic farmers had at least five species. This may be a component of the high yields found among the organic farms (see chapter 8). Oddly, highly diverse systems were slightly more common in transi-

TABLE 9.1

Number of shade species by technology (percent)

Number of species	0–2	3–4	5–6	7 or more
Chemical (N=11)	9	46	36	9
Transition (N= 25)	4	40	40	16
Organic (N=42)	10	21	29	40
Natural (N=12)	0	33	29	38

Note: figures represent the percentage of all farmers, for each type of technology, with up to the given number of shade species in their coffee grove. N=90.

tional and organic settings than in those with natural technology, perhaps as a result of the strong promotion of diversity on the part of those organizations that are devoted to organic farming.

EROSION: THE EFFECTS OF SLOPE AND TERRACES

In the broken terrain of Chiapas, erosion is a critical indicator of the long-term sustainability of production. This study found a highly significant positive linear relationship between erosion and degree of slope.[4] Because this relationship is well known, it has been common on coffee plantations to construct terraces whenever coffee is planted on steep slopes. In fact, terraces are required for organic certification (Dardón 1995; IFOAM 1995). They are supposed to function to slow erosion and to promote better soil quality and water retention, though producers often complain that the labor required is excessive and they do not function well. There are two kinds of terraces: small ones for each individual plant and long ones, which follow slope contours. This study found no statistical relationship whatsoever between either kind of terrace and erosion,[5] supporting their detractors' assertions as well as other studies (see, e.g., Perezgrovas 1996). In short, the construction of individual terraces does not appear to be a fruitful way to invest in improving natural capital.

For those farmers who used living barriers[6] instead of terraces, the erosion was much lower, though there were not enough cases for a conclusive statistical analysis. Nevertheless, this finding is highly suggestive and worthy of further examination, especially as living barriers require far less labor to construct and maintain than terraces. (see Perezgrovas 1996). Eliminating the requirement of terraces for certification might not only make conversion to organic more attractive to farmers but result in higher profit as well as lowering labor costs (see AICA 1997).

EROSION ACROSS VARIOUS FARMING TECHNOLOGIES

A simple statistical analysis of erosion on farms with each type of technology revealed that those that employed natural technology had less erosion than the other systems (the relationship is almost significant; see figure 9.2).[7] This makes sense because, unlike the other methods, natural technology leaves the ground relatively undisturbed; no soil is moved in the process of weeding or terrace construction. And moving soil increases the likelihood of erosion. As we shall see below, there is also greater coverage of the soil with leaf litter in the natural system. This is an area that farmers need to work on, though it is also worth noting that the smaller-scale chemical farmers like those in this study have more shade, and thus more leaf litter, than do large-scale chemical farmers.

In order to discover as many of the causal factors behind erosion as possible, I carried out an exploratory statistical analysis for all the vari-

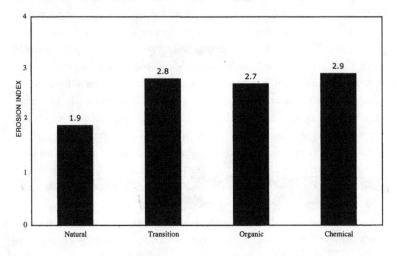

$p = .13, N = 86$

Figure 9.2. Erosion index by technology

ables measured,[8] to determine which would be related to erosion and how. Those variables that were included in the highly significant model[9] were slope, technology, and the proportion of the ground covered by leaf litter and humus. The final model was:

$$\text{Erosion Index (1–4)} = 1.6 + 0.4(\text{slope}) - 0.2(\text{leaf litter index}) - 0.9(\text{natural technology})$$

where natural technology is a dummy variable taking on values of 1 or 0 (the farmer either uses natural technology or doesn't use it). Slope appears to be the driving force, mitigated by keeping the ground covered with leaf litter and humus and the use of natural technology.

LEAF LITTER AND HUMUS

Coverage by leaf litter or humus was chosen as the final ecological indicator. In this study, this indicator was estimated both as an index of the proportion of the ground covered and by the average depth of the leaf litter/humus layer. Leaf litter coverage varied significantly by technology; chemical technology had the least coverage, and natural the most, followed closely by organic and transitional (figure 9.3). This finding reinforces the

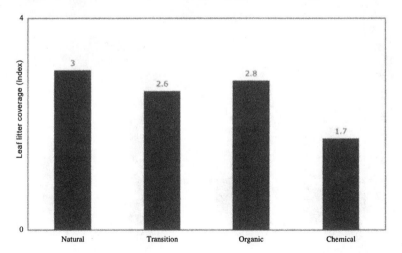

Figure 9.3. Leaf litter coverage by technology. *Note:* Index (1–4) is proportion of ground covered by leaf litter and humus. $p < .01$, $N = 86$.

role of natural technology in stemming soil erosion and probably is a positive indication for transitional and organic methods as well.

What is truly remarkable are the results for the average *depth* of the leaf litter and humus layer, a key indicator of future soil fertility. Here there was a very significant relationship with technology. The average depth on organic (7.2 cm) plots was nearly double that of natural and transitional (both 4.6 cm), which in turn had greater average depth than chemical plots (3.2 cm) (figure 9.4). Organic practices thus appear to be seriously improving the soil, lending support to the notion that the process of conversion to organic is a real investment in building natural capital for the future.

Organic Farming: Good Investment Made Possible by Social Capital

The data presented in this chapter and the previous one clearly demonstrates how *investment* in natural capital, via conversion to organic, the introduction of shade biodiversity, and the buildup of leaf litter and humus, pay off in productive (yield) and economic (gross income) terms,

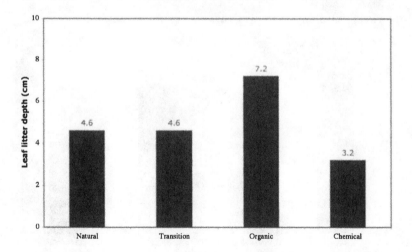

$p < .01, N = 86$

Figure 9.4. Average depth of leaf litter and humus layer, by technology

as well as in the future sustainability of production (erosion prevention, future soil fertility). Clearly these factors make the investment in natural capital through organic farming a viable alternative for coffee farmers to the intensification of production through chemical methods. Part of the economic payoff from the investment in organic farming comes through the *internalization* of its environmental benefits to society at large, via certification and price premiums (for a discussion of the internalization of benefits, see chapter 6). Furthermore, a key advantage of organic farming under the conditions found in Chiapas is that it provides a Chayanovian mechanism to turn underutilized family labor into income—a factor that might even provide an alternative to out-migration and the community breakdown it generates.

The payoffs from the internalization of environmental benefits would be impossible without the earlier formation of significant social capital, because only effective organizations are able to obtain and maintain certification in the organic market. Given the amount of technical assistance provided by these organizations to the farmers who are undergoing the transition to organic, by either professional staff or by campesino promoters, and the organizational learning involved, it is unlikely that even the natural capital investment of converting to organic could have been undertaken without having had sufficient social capital already in place. Thus, we can perhaps identify three cycles of social capital formation among coffee producers in Chiapas as follows:

- Cycle 1: Organizations are built under tutelage of state institutions.
- Cycle 2: Structural adjustment and neoliberalism wean them from state tutelage; some of them become stronger as a result, and are able to survive the reconfiguration of the coffee economy. A key step taken by some organizations here is to use the social capital they have formed as a platform for natural capital investment strategies.
- Cycle 3: The terrain shifts due to the Zapatista rebellion, creating new external allies for some, at the same time as coffee prices plunge, leading more organizations to pursue natural capital strategies in order to benefit from the internalization of benefits via price premiums.

Clearly, there are differences between organizations reflected in the data presented here as well—differences in technological strategies, in how technical assistance is provided, in the attention given to ecological enhancement, food security, and other nonfarming issues, and in the priority placed on coffee versus other crops and other economic activities. Nevertheless, it is clear that for many of these organizations, the social capital accumulated in the 1970s, 1980s, and 1990s left them with the organizational capacity necessary to take advantage of the opportunities that opened for them with the growth of the organic market.

Chapter 10

Conclusions

Sustainable Development by Mayan Farmers

CENTURIES OF EUROPEAN colonial domination marked the entry into the global capitalist system of most countries from the south. Immense extensions of land were stolen, and native populations were forced to produce the products demanded by the metropolis. One such product was coffee, around which the dependent economies of many states in the tropics were developed.

Coffee Production and Markets

Coffee is different from other third world export crops in that the production and processing technologies involved were mostly developed in producing countries themselves. Thus coffee contributed greatly to the formation of states and to building modern infrastructure, because it allowed for more capital accumulation in producing countries than did other export crops. Coffee continues to be an important source of foreign exchange for many countries, including Mexico. It is produced by both large and small farmers, using three principal categories of production technologies.

Natural coffee technology is the province of those small producers who do not put a lot of labor into their plots and provide minimum maintenance.

In the traditional growing strategy, coffee plants are randomly planted within a diverse canopy of shade trees, many of which yield useful products themselves. This method depends on detailed knowledge of the pattern of plant growth in particular environments.

Organic production is an intensive form of traditional production and has similar characteristics. The vegetative structure of either traditional or organic production features several layers of tree canopy that provide shade for the coffee plants. The presence of diverse shade species creates a stable production system that provides protection from soil erosion, fosters favorable local temperatures and humidity regimes, ensures constant replenishment of the soil's organic matter via leaf litter production, and encourages an array of beneficial insects that act to control potential pests.

Organic farming methods are similar to those of traditional production in that shade is used. They also resemble those of more technified production in that there is more intensive use of inputs, although organic inputs and human labor are substituted for the agrochemicals used in chemical methods. Together with natural production, organic is considered to be one of the most stable and ecologically sound agroforestry systems in Mesoamerica.

Technified production of coffee involves the use of high-yielding varieties of seeds, agrochemical inputs, and the reduction of shade. Shade trees are partially or completely removed and replaced with new sun-tolerant coffee hybrids planted in open rows along slopes, while the use of purchased chemical inputs like fertilizers, herbicides, and fungicides is intensified. Technification introduced low-stature, compact varieties, and planting density on such plantations changed from two meters between plants (as in traditional coffee) to only thirty-five to forty centimeters. The new varieties of plants respond rapidly to chemical inputs such as fertilizer and are very sun tolerant. Without shade, weeds proliferate, so this technology also must rely heavily on herbicides.

Due to the technification of the production process in some Latin American countries, coffee went from being an exception among export crops, in that it had a low reliance on imported inputs, to one that depends heavily on agrochemicals. However, in Mexico and especially Chiapas, complete technification was done only by large and some medium producers. What is called chemical production in this book is practiced by small farmers who have only partially adopted the technification model.

Their production is characterized by the use of agrochemicals and re-duced shade diversity and shade coverage.

Regardless of production methods, the coffee economy is heavily de-pendent on the international market. For many years this market was heav-ily regulated by the International Coffee Agreement (ICA), which sought to balance the interests of exporting and importing countries, and by na-tional coffee institutes in exporting countries, which provided a range of critical services to coffee farmers and participated directly or indirectly in the marketing chain. The Mexican Coffee Institute (INMECAFE) was a major source of support for small coffee producers since it was in charge of research, support, credit, storage, and distribution. However, IN-MECAFE promoted the use of agrochemicals among small producers and the technification of the coffee groves following a science-based model of natural capital use.

In recent years the national and international coffee markets have been drastically reconfigured. In 1989 the ICA collapsed and the futures market began to set world prices with a new quality-based pricing system. This change opened new opportunities for small producers, at the same time as they were faced with the loss of critical services when INMECAFE was shut down as a part of Mexico's structural adjustment program. Coffee from small-farmer cooperatives, "shade coffee," "bird-friendly coffee," and organic coffee are some examples of the growing market segmentation and differentiation of the *specialty* and *gourmet* coffee markets that are in-creasingly being exploited by small producers.

Another outlet for small coffee producers has been created by alterna-tive trade organizations (ATOs) and the fair trade movement. Alternative trade addresses the inequity of the terms of trade in which the north sets prices and producers in the south have to accept them. ATOs seek to transform conditions of poverty in rural areas by providing poor peasants with new marketing channels, technical assistance, and better prices through consumer's buying power in northern countries. Fair trade is part of the alternative trade movement and has focused on coffee based on a minimum of US$1.21 per pound plus 5 cents for social projects, and $1.41 for organic coffee.

The reconfiguration of the market has represented an opportunity for small producers that produce high-quality coffee, especially those pro-ducing organically. As these opportunities have opened in the market, small farmers have been able to take advantage of them, as long as they are well organized and produce with quality. Their high level of social capital is the key element that allows them to tap into these market opportunities.

Social and Natural Capital in Rural Development

Social capital refers to the nature and intensity of relationships established between members of civil society. The relationships, networks, and trust that civil society—defined as organization beyond the family circle—engages in are all part of social capital. These are resources that facilitate the actions of individuals who are part of the same network or organization.

Jonathan Fox (1996) has proposed a theory of recursive cycles of social capital formation between the state and societal actors. Civil society, authoritarian elites, and reformist allies within the state or civil society are the main participants in these recursive cycles. A cycle begins with an event such as an economic crisis, war, popular protest, or political succession that divides the elite into those arguing for either political legitimacy (negotiating) or coercion (repression). Social organizations tend to demand broader access to the state when these divisions occur, and such organizations may be protected from repression by reformist allies either inside the state or within broader—national or international—civil society. Eventually, the cycle closes with an authoritarian backlash, and if the social organization manages to conserve its autonomy, it will use that autonomy for the next political opportunity. Elites play a key role in allowing reformists to open political spaces for grassroots organizations. These cycles can be seen quite clearly in the history of small-farmer coffee organizations in Chiapas, where ethnic identity is frequently being used to strengthen social capital and the market position of grassroots cooperatives.

The recent success of the coffee organizations passing through these cycles was in part due to a strategy of investment in their natural resources or natural capital. Natural capital includes all the components of the ecosphere and the relationships among them that form and regenerate natural resources and provide environmental services. Natural capital has three environmental functions: provision of resources (renewable, nonrenewable, cultivated) for production, absorption of waste from production (either positively, as recycling or fertilization, or negatively, as polluting or eroding) and environmental services (climate and ecosystem stability). There is no single way of measuring the value of the environmental services provided by natural capital.

Natural capital can be increased or diminished by human activity. Erosion, for example, decreases natural capital; investments are a conscious way of increasing it. Water and soil conservation practices increase natural capital, protect the environment, and help reduce poverty. In fact, human societies have used a variety of natural capital-based strategies.

Yet, services provided from, or costs of, natural capital, have not in the past been taken into account in cost-benefit analyses of development projects. Examining the costs of pollution and depletion of resources by development projects would provide a very different picture of the dominant fossil fuel–based development model. On the other hand, paying for the environmental services provided by the good management of natural resources by poor people could contribute to poverty reduction and enhancement of the environment.

Cultivated natural capital, or agriculture, has been carried out in diverse manners, ranging from low-input practices based on traditional knowledge to high-technology agricultural production dependent on chemical inputs and machinery. So-called science-based agriculture has been promoted all over Latin America by governments and agrochemical companies as *the* way to intensify production. The use of external inputs like chemical pesticides and fertilizers, machines, and large-scale irrigation to boost food production characterizes these ways of using natural capital, which, rather than building up stocks of natural assets, actually depreciate them through soil erosion and loss of functional biodiversity. The typical results are the generalized loss of biodiversity, compacted, eroded, and degraded soils, pollution of groundwater, and economic concentration and exclusion of poor farmers. In sum, renewable and nonrenewable natural capital are thus depleted.

Sustainable agriculture technologies provide an alternative to intensify production while building and regenerating natural capital. Agroecological and organic management practices are an alternative method of intensification of agriculture that represent good investments in natural capital. This type of technology seeks to integrate natural processes (nutrient cycling, nitrogen fixation, pest-predator relationships, etc.) into agricultural production with the minimization of external inputs and the full participation of farmers using their local knowledge. These labor-intensive investments can enhance wildlife and the management of watersheds, as well as helping to maintain and increase biodiversity. The current challenge is to make better use of natural resources by minimizing the use of external inputs and regenerating resources.

When we take a broad look at agricultural development processes, we can see crucial roles played by both social and natural capital. The relationships, organizations, and networks that make up social capital are the essential first ingredient in development. Connections within and between communities on a local, regional, national, or international level supply the necessary contacts to push development forward. Strategies that are based on investment in natural capital require the prior formation of social capital, but can, in turn, contribute significantly to the rural development process. Associations of small coffee producers provide an excellent case study for examining these processes in the larger search for more sustainable development.

Social capital grew extensively in rural Mexico over the last few decades through a number of recursive cycles. In several of these cycles reformist government officials recognized and encouraged relatively autonomous grassroots organizations, and coffee producers played an important role in these processes. Although reformist allies buffered organizations from repression for a while, each cycle was closed by an authoritarian backlash. The cumulative effect of social organization in these cycles characterizes social capital formation in rural Mexico.

In Chiapas these cycles also took place in the context of the reconfiguration of the coffee market. In the first cycle, the state helped producers form associations in order to participate in development programs. IN-MECAFE was the most important state agency for coffee producers at that time; it organized producers into Unidades Económicas de Producción y Comercialización (UEPCs).

The Unión de Uniones de Ejidos was formed during the 1970s and eventually gave rise to the Unión de Ejidos de la Selva, an organization that focused on the commercialization of coffee for those who had won land in previous struggles. The Majomut cooperative began with the support of state reformists in the National Indigenous Institute (INI). These allies were crucial for its initial organization. Communities with different political allegiances were part of Majomut from the beginning, and today

Majomut is tolerant of diverse political affiliations and religious practices. This quality has given the organization strength.

The Unión de Credito Pajal Yakaltik was formed in the cycle of the 1980s and later split into several new organizations, including the Tzotzilotic Tzobolotic cooperative. Half its members became Zapatistas and left the organization in the 1990s. MutVitz was supported by the international solidarity movement in support of the Zapatistas. Their success is building as they take advantage of solidarity markets. ISMAM was formed with religious allies who were looking for economic alternatives for their faithful. A key individual was a priest-advisor who provided leadership by working alongside the cooperative members. They have achieved a significant scale that allows them to buffer repression, and they are run quite democratically.

The myriad of small cooperatives in Chiapas demonstrate how the ability to "scale up" is critical in the coffee-producing social sector. Without having achieved regional scope, these organizations have not been able to successfully tap into the international market.

Overall, the state played a significant role in starting most of the organizations in this study (especially, but not only, in the 1970s). Structural adjustment and the shrinking of the state then forced them to wean themselves from state support and appropriate the production process (1980s), strengthening social capital in the process. The 1990s created the possibility of a new external ally—Zapatista solidarity—which helped get a new organization (MutVitz) started. In this cycle we also saw how the social capital built up in Chiapas allowed many organizations to survive the crash in coffee prices by going organic and taking advantage of fair trade opportunities.

Only the formation of significant social capital allowed these coffee farmers to navigate the changing terrain of the national and global coffee market in the wake of the breakup of the ICA and the disappearance of INMECAFE. The farmers were truly forced to "appropriate the production process" once INMECAFE stopped offering technical assistance, transport, and marketing. With the social capital they developed, they were then able to take advantage of the niches that opened in the global market with the collapse of the ICA. More specifically, their enormous success with, indeed the boom of, organic coffee, would have been impossible without substantial previous buildup of social capital. It would be way too costly—impossible, in fact—for unorganized small-scale farmers to obtain, or pay for, organic (or fair trade) certification. And only well-organized co-ops are capable of the internal controls needed for keeping their certification.

Investments in Organic Farming and Sustainability

In fact, these organizations have, over their brief history, engaged in all the principal routes to building natural capital, or natural assets (with the exception of Lázaro Cárdenas). Some degree of *redistribution* took place earlier under various versions of agrarian reform, as well as the *appropriation* of land via social mobilization. What the data presented in this study demonstrate most clearly, however, is how *investments* in natural assets, via conversion to organic, the introduction of shade biodiversity, and the buildup of leaf litter and humus, have paid off in both productive (yield) and economic (gross income) terms, and in terms of ecological indicators of the future sustainability of production (erosion prevention, future soil fertility, etc.). Clearly, the strategy of investment in natural capital by organic farming is a viable alternative to chemicals in terms of the intensification of coffee agriculture. Part of the economic payoff to these investments comes via the *internalization* of the environmental benefits of organic farming to society at large, via certification and price premiums.

Sustainable development should be economically viable, socially just, and ecologically sound, in the sense both of not damaging the external environment and of conserving or enhancing the resource base for future production. In general terms, *socially just* means a broader distribution of the benefits of development, but in the case of coffee production technologies, we can consider *socially just* as referring to those options that are more appropriate for poorer farmers. Thus the lower investment of natural technology, and the alternative route to intensification based on applying more labor and enhancing natural assets by organic farming, would be favored over the more capital-intensive chemical approach (especially under conditions like those in much of rural Chiapas, where there is a low opportunity cost for family labor). The data on the outcomes of the different technological options evaluated here, then, allow us to examine the remaining two dimensions of sustainability. We can use yield (productivity) and gross income as proxies for economic viability (and to some extent for social justice), and erosion, ground cover, depth of leaf litter and humus, and shade biodiversity as indicators of ecological sustainability. In figure 10.1 the values of these parameters are plotted graphically on radar, or kite, graphs as a visual display of the relative sustainability of the four technological approaches.

In such a graph, the larger the area covered by the diagram, the more sustainable the system is (Monzote, Muñoz, and Funes-Monzote 2002).

Natural

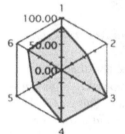

Transitional

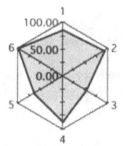

Organic   **Chemical**

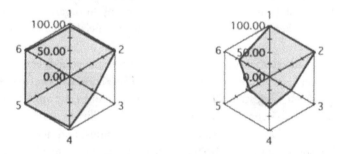

Legend: 1 = corrected yield; 2 = gross income/ha; 3 = erosion index (inverse); 4 = ground cover index; 5 = depth of leaf litter/humus; 6 = average number of shade species.

Figure 10.1. Indicators of sustainability. *Note:* All indicators have been placed on a relative scale of 0 to 100.

One can see the advantages of the organic approach quite clearly in this way. It is equal or superior to the other three in all dimensions except soil erosion—where natural technology is superior—and even here one might imagine that organic's superior ground coverage with leaf litter might, over time, give it an advantage. Seen this way, organic farming of coffee bests natural technology in economic terms and it is superior to chemical technology in ecological terms, providing the best overall combination of productivity today, plus the likely sustainability of that productivity into the future. If we add to that the advantages mentioned above in terms of socially just criteria, then it would be fair to conclude that overall the organic approach—which is based on investing in natural capital and internalizing benefits to society—is the most *sustainable* option.

The Interaction between Social and Natural Capital

The payoffs from investing in natural capital and the internalization of benefits—via a price premium—would be impossible to obtain without the earlier formation of significant social capital. This is partially because only effective organizations are able to obtain and maintain certification in the organic market. Furthermore, given the amount of technical assistance provided by these organizations to the farmers who are undergoing the transition to organic, by either professional staff or by campesino-promoters, and the organizational learning involved, it is unlikely that even the natural capital investment of converting to organic could have been undertaken without having had sufficient social capital already in place.

The present dedication to organic coffee among small-farmer organizations in Chiapas can be seen as providing alternatives to poverty and to environmental degradation. Poverty reduction and environmental enhancement both depend on these organizations' ability to develop significant social capital. The relationships, organizations, and networks that make up social capital have been essential to the ability of small producers to survive and navigate the changing terrain of the reconfigured coffee economy.

Yet if their organizations did not also have a strategy of investing in natural capital and internalizing benefits, small farmers would be in the desperate situation now facing many larger and more technified producers. These highly capitalized plantation owners (not examined in this book) are facing prices for their conventional, nonorganic coffee that are so low that in some cases they do not even cover the cost of hiring labor for the harvest, and their coffee groves are so degraded by erosion and by the effects of too much sunlight on their coffee plants—the product of having drastically reduced or eliminated shade—that their productivity is plunging (Eduardo Martínez, pers. comm., 2000). Because of this crisis some of these large growers are now abandoning coffee altogether. On the other hand, small farmers, equipped with social capital, were able to follow a different path, which was to invest in natural capital. This has slowed or prevented the degradation of their coffee groves. Social capital has also enabled them to internalize the larger benefits to society of their more ecologically sound practices, getting the organic price market premium as well as gaining access to the fair trade market. The combined strategy followed by many small-farmer organizations, of social capital formation and investment in natural capital, can actually improve their groves instead of degrading them, and moves them into a market niche where prices are better. Thus we may conclude that organic farming is a viable approach toward more sustainable rural development.

Notes

Chapter 2

1. All names used in quotations from interviews are pseudonyms, to protect confidentiality.

2. This approach uses greater air flow and penetration of sunlight to combat coffee rust—a fungus called *roya* in Spanish—that usually affects the arabica varieties.

3. See the work of Robert Rice (2003) about the effects of this crisis in Central America.

4. Sometimes young children are not allowed because they are not old enough to help and, because of the food they consume, become a cost to the finca owners.

5. For a detailed study on organization of work among producers and workers, see the work of Deborah Sick, 1999.

Chapter 3

1. The ICA was first broken from 1972 to 1980, due to the devaluation of the dollar in 1971 and the importer countries' refusal to renegotiate prices. The second suspension was from March 1986 to September 1987, due to a drought in Brazil, the biggest producer country, that led to high prices (Restrepo 1990).

2. Efforts to include other products have grown recently. For the case of bananas, see Murray and Raynolds 1998, 2000.

3. EFTA is also the acronym for the European Free Trade Association.

4. The findings for Canada, Mexico, and the United States were 22, 19, and 21 percent, respectively.

5. Caffeine can be removed from coffee using a variety of solvents, including methylene chloride, ethyl acetate, or water. Water is sometimes combined with a carbon dioxide pressure treatment. The water-based methods are preferable. For more information, see http://science.howstuffworks.com/question480.htm.

Chapter 4

1. First introduced by the Spanish in the nineteenth century, the finca was a large private agricultural plantation. In Central America today, *finca* means a farm of any size; in Chiapas the term continues to be associated with larger units of production.

2. Huehuetan was an important Pipil town. It became the second capital of Soconusco after the first capital, near the town of Escuintla, was destroyed by a hurricane (Otto Schumann, pers. comm., 2001).

3. The present language of the Tuzantecos is a variation of Motozintleco or Mocho. Tuzanteco is a defunct language, as is Tapachulteco (Schumann 1969).

4. Matías Romero's *Cultivo meridional del café en la costa meridional de Chiapas* (1893) contained all the instructions needed for running a coffee plantation, including most of the recommendations found in more recent manuals (e.g., Sánchez 1990; Martínez and Peters 1994). The guide described all the region's climatological conditions and all the steps in the production process, stressed the importance of shade in cultivation, and included an economic analysis of coffee production.

5. The Mexican government gave the first concession to the Compañía Mexicana de Colonización de San Francisco and later to the Chiapas Land and Colonization Company Ltd., which promoted settlement. The sierra and jungle regions were not part of the concession, and therefore those regions were colonized by Mexicans and Guatemalans.

6. In 1882 Guatemala recognized the area of Márquez de Comillas as part of Mexico but continued making territorial claims on Chiapas until 1895 (Cortés 1998).

7. It was difficult for the workers to organize with common interests, because the finca owners gave their workers permission to cultivate small parcels of land for subsistence purposes. Thus while the finca workers shared a common fate as wage workers, they also depended on the finca owners for their individual subsistence. Another complexity was that the workers who came only for the harvest had a strong sense of identity as farm workers, but when they returned to their land they became campesinos again (Pohlenz 1995).

8. Through the cargo system, married men serve their communities by doing specific community jobs for a year (policeman, alcalde, judge, organizer of the religious fiesta, etc.). A cargo implies considerable expenditures to fulfill the obligations of office, which in turn accumulate prestige within the community.

9. It is estimated that eight hundred thousand hectares are deforested each year in Mexico (Centro de Ecología 1997). A vast literature exists on the problems of conservation and development in the Lacandón jungle. See, for example, Alvarez del Toro 1975; Bray 1997; Carr 2000; Centro de Ecología 1997; Cortés 1998; González Ponciano 1995; Toledo, Batis, et al. 1995; Toledo, Ortiz-Espejel, et al. 2003. A poster series was created as part of an interdisciplinary research project to promote conservation among the inhabitants of the jungle region (Arizpe, Paz, and Velázquez 1993).

10. Mexico has been an example of community-based forest management, but in the Lacandón area the management has been by the government (Bray 1997).

11. The cañadas (valleys) zone is divided into two regions, according to their different geographical characteristics and histories of colonization. The Ocosingo-Altamirano cañadas have two-thirds of the population of the entire zone (96,000 in 1991), most of whom are Tzeltal Mayans; the remaining third, mostly Tojolabal Mayans, inhabits the Margaritas cañada (Toledo, Ortiz-Espejel, et al. 2003).

12. According to González Ponciano (1995, cited in Harvey 1998), between 1982 and 1984 there were ten thousand Mexicans in these thirteen ejidos and there were eighteen thousand Guatemalan refugees. By 1986 the Mexican population was twenty-two thousand, and most of the refugees had been relocated to the states of Campeche and Quintana Roo (Harvey 1998).

Chapter 5

1. The concept of social capital originated in the social sciences. The concept borrows the idea of capital from economics, while extending it into non-monetary spheres of life. Robert Putnam (1993) terms the networks, norms, and trust among members of civil society "social capital." The work of Putnam and a group of political scientists studying civic participation and regional government performance in Italy marked the appearance of the social capital concept in development discourse (Harriss and De Renzio 1997).

2. The Coordinadora Nacional Plan de Ayala was founded in 1979 to focus on agrarian reform in affiliation with parties on the left, but it recently moved to be more independent of any political party influence.

3. When it was founded in 1963, the Central Independiente de Obreros Agrícolas y Campesinos was affiliated with the Mexican Communist Party (PCM). Later it broke in two and one part affiliated with the official Revolutionary

Institutional Party (PRI). The second group was reorganized in 1976 by Ramón Danzos Palomino and recovered the original name, CIOAC.

4. The Unión Nacional de Organizaciones Regionales Campesinas Autónomas was founded in 1985 through the coordination of twenty-five campesino organizations with different political affiliations.

5. The term *mestizo* refers to a person of mixed European and indigenous ancestry, or to a person in Mexico whose self-identity is nonindigenous.

Chapter 6

1. Sidney Tarrow (1996) postulates that it is good government that leads to the creation of social capital. He emphasizes the great influence that state institutions have in shaping norms, networks, and social organizations. Judith Tendler (1997), however, argues that better governance comes out of positive synergisms between closely interacting civil society organizations, local governments, *and* central governments. She found that the causal relationships between civil society and good governance are far from being unidirectional.

2. In a contrastive analysis, Putnam and colleagues (1993) concluded that the north of Italy had developed more than the south because they found a stronger presence of "civic engagement networks," or interacting civic organizations, in the north. Putnam's analysis of social capital density included every organization from soccer clubs and unions to newspaper readership and participation in civic institutions as indicators of the vibrancy of associational life.

3. This is analogous to the restrictions on individual freedom and business initiative that some norms and obligations impose on individuals, as described by Alejandro Portes and Patricia Landolt (1996). In the same vein, Tewodaj Mogues and Michael R. Carter (2004) highlight the negative effects that social capital can have in highly polarized situations.

4. Natural capital has been discussed mainly in environmental economics circles, when an attempt is made to calculate the value of services that ecosystems provide. E. F. Schumacher (1983) first used the term *natural capital* when warning economists that fossil fuels should be treated as depreciable natural capital. That is, the amount of oil or coal available on the planet can be viewed as a capital stock that can be drawn down, depleted, or depreciated by usage rates that exceed the rates of formation of new oil reserves or coal beds. Robert Costanza and colleagues (1997) have estimated an average value of US$33 trillion per year provided by seventeen ecosystem services (calculated in 1997 dollars). The quantification and measurement of natural capital

stocks, and their loss, is very difficult, according to ecological economist Juan Martínez Alier (1995). He argues that natural phenomena cannot be reduced to mere numbers and recommends the use of biological, physical, economic, and social indicators in research and monitoring in order to gain an understanding of the processes that bring about the degradation of nature. Martínez Alier and Martin O'Connor state that the "prices of environmental resources and services formed by transactions among humans who are alive at present will depend on the existence (or nonexistence) and the endowment of property rights on 'natural capital,' and they will also depend on the distribution of income already within the present generation of humans" (1996, 155). Some scholars of ecological economics have attempted to integrate social aspects into the definition of natural capital (e.g., Gupta 1996; Leff 1996; Martínez and O'Connor 1996).

5. Friedrich Hinterberger, Fred Luks, and Friedrich Schmidt-Bleek (1997) and Martin O'Connor (1994) are among a number of scholars who have criticized the concept of natural capital for commodifying nature. While Hinterberger and his colleagues accept that both conventional capital (money) and natural capital can be considered as stocks that can be saved for the future, the word *capital* implies that nature can be produced by human beings. In economic terms, capital can be thought of either as a cash fund that circulates or as replaceable stocks—characteristics that, they argue, do not apply to natural capital.

6. Some believe it is necessary to intensify traditional agriculture so that agricultural production can meet the future needs of a growing world population, an argument that is essentially Malthusian (Avery 1995; I. Carruthers 1993; DowElanco 1994; Knutson et al. 1990). Others believe that traditional agriculture intensifies as a response to increases in population density from either growth or migration (Boserup 1965; Geertz 1963). Seen from the perspective of poor farmers with limited access to land, intensification can also be viewed as a route to the generation of more income or income savings or both, as well as a route to poverty reduction (Pretty 1997).

Chapter 7

1. A *municipio* (municipality) is the political administrative unit of all Mexican states. Depending on their size they may include several communities, towns, and perhaps one city.

2. This is very similar in any agricultural activity, such as the documented process of conversion to cattle ranching (*ganaderización*) in Veracruz (Lazos 1996).

3. The German-Mexican family owner was influenced by the Rudolph Steiner biodynamics philosophy. They acquired the finca from an Irish family in 1965 (Martínez and Peters 1995).

4. The few studies of the difficulties of reconciling the differences between advisors and campesinos demonstrate the significance of those cultural differences. Gisela Landazuri (1997) defines the interaction as a dynamic space for negotiating experiences, identities, and changing power relationships. She also observes that the interaction consists of nonverbal language and discourse as well as concrete actions. She concludes that this interaction is the expression of distinct rationalities. She emphasizes an understanding of rural development that takes such interpersonal factors into account. In current practice, she observes, "the cultural distance between the subjects is ignored or denied. One must take the attitude of opening up in which listening, eye contact and even qualities such as intuition and perception are tools for constructing rural development from the social subjects themselves" (13).

5. The agrarian communities of Chenalhó, Panthelò, Cancuc, and the ejidos Los Chorros and Puebla.

6. Forania is an administrative unit of the Catholic Church.

7. Tequio, from the Nahuatl "tequitl" meaning work or tribute, was the work imposed on the Indians as tribute to the Spanish. The term continues to be used to designate the work done to benefit the community.

8. Later became the Fair Trade Organization group working on fair trade in the Netherlands.

9. The Unión de Ejidos de Tenejapa, the Sociedad Cooperativa Tiemenlola, and the Unión de Ejidos Juan Sabines.

Chapter 8

1. In this case a simple analysis of variance (ANOVA) for the 110 cases where yield estimates were obtained in the interviews (averaged over years to reduce variation).

2. In this study the quantitative data from the questionnaires were analyzed using stepwise multiple regression. Dummy or indicator variables (with a value or 1 or 0) were used for those variables that take the form of yes/no (or present/absent) and for qualitative variables (for example, if one of three qualitatively different, discontinuous types of soil preparation was used). Biological, social, economic, ecological, and agronomic reasoning was used in choosing which variables to include at the beginning of each stepwise multiple regression, and the regression process was used to choose the model with

the most explanatory ability. Curvilinear responses were checked for, when the above-mentioned forms of reasoning warranted it (see Kleinbaum, Lawrence, Mulher, and Nizam 1997).

3. Readers who are interested in data for yield and the other variables reported in this book analyzed by organization should refer to Martinez-Torres (2003).

4. Note that the figure is given in gross income. The cost of production is not deducted from this amount. The cost is presumably higher in the chemical technology than in the rest.

Chapter 9

1. Given the difficulty and inherent unreliability of the methods available for measuring erosion with precision (Deinlein 1993), a visual index was selected as the indicator of erosion. The coffee parcel was examined for signs of erosion (bare soil, rills, gullies) while walking with the farmer, in order to classify the degree of erosion observed as None, Little, Medium, or High (with intermediate points between the four degrees).

2. The indicator of soil quality was the average depth of leaf litter/humus as measured with a ruler at ten different randomly chosen points across each parcel regardless of parcel size. Leaf litter/humus is the first step toward restoring organic matter to the soil in order to maintain natural fertility (Parra and Díaz 1997; Perfecto and Vandermeer 1994), and thus offers a good fertility-related indicator of sustainability. The points were chosen in a stratified random pattern across the whole parcel. The producer was asked to guide the investigator to the four corners of his parcel and a marker was tossed backward to randomly choose points which were stratified across the parcel. These were the points where the depth measurements were taken.

3. The principal source of vegetative diversity within a producing coffee grove is found in the species of trees that provide shade (Plaza Sanchez 1997; Perfecto, Rice, Greenberg, and Van der Voort 1996; Rice and Ward 1997). Thus the indicator used for biodiversity was based on the number of different shade tree species found in the grove, a value obtained by a combination of visual inspection and questions to the farmer.

4. $p < .001$, $r^2 = 0.33$. Erosion Index = 0.27 + 0.41 (index of slope). The erosion index can have any whole number value between 1 and 4.

5. $p > .05$.

6. Living barriers consist of perennials planted along contour lines to slow erosion.

7. In a later analysis in this chapter, where more variables are controlled for, this relationship is found to be significant.

8. Stepwise multiple regression. Refer to Martinez-Torres (2003) for the details of this and the other statistical analyses presented here.

9. $p < .001$; $R^2 = 0.44$.

Bibliography

Agarwal, Bina. 1992. The gender and environment debate: Lessons from India. *Feminist Studies* 18 (1): 119–58.

AICA (Agencia Informativa Católica Argentina). 1997. Evaluación del programa de producción de café orgánico de Las Margaritas, Chiapas, México. Final report, Mexico City.

Altieri, Miguel A. 1995. *Agroecology: The science of sustainable agriculture.* Boulder: Westview.

———. 1996. Hacia un concepto de salud agroecologica. In *Ecología aplicada a la agricultura: Temas selectos de México,* comp. J. Trujillo Arriaga, F. de León González, R. Calderón Arozqueta, and P. Torres Lima. Mexico City: Universidad Autónoma Metropolitana/Unidad Xochimilco, 13–14.

———. 1999. Enhancing the productivity of Latin American traditional peasant farming systems through an agroecological approach. Paper presented at the International Conference on Sustainable Agriculture: An Evaluation of New Paradigms and Old Practices, Bellagio Center, Bellagio, Italy, April 26–30.

Altieri, M. A., and O. Masera. 1993. Sustainable rural development in Latin America: Building from the bottom up. *Ecological Economics* 7: 93–121.

Alvarez del Toro, Miguel. 1975. Panorama ecológico del estado. In *Chiapas y sus recursos naturales renovables,* edited by INAREMAC. Serie de mesas redondas. Mexico City: Instituto Mexicano de Recursos Naturales Renovables.

Alvarez Simán, F. 1996. *Capitalismo, el estado y el campesino en México: Un estudio sobre la región del Soconusco en Chiapas.* Mexico City: Universidad Autónoma de Chiapas.

Arenas Melo, Martha Lucía. 1981. *Factores que afectan la comercialización del café.* Bogotá: ANIF, Fondo Editorial.

Arizpe, Lourdes, Fernanda Paz, and Margarita Velázquez. 1998. *Culture and global change: Social perceptions of deforestation in the Lacandona Rain Forest in Mexico.* Ann Arbor: University of Michigan Press.

Avery, Dennis. 1995. *Saving the planet with pesticides and plastic: The environmental triumph of high-yield farming.* Indianapolis: Hudson Institute.

Badstue, L. B., M. R. Bellón, X. Juárez, I. M. Rosas, and A. M. Solano. 2002. Social relations and seed transactions among small-scale maize farmers in the central valleys of Oaxaca, Mexico: Preliminary findings. CIMMYT Economics Working Paper 02–02. Mexico City: CIMMYT.

Bancomex (Banco de México), 2002. Café: Tendencias y perspectivas de exportación. Bancomex Commodity Report. Mexico City: Banco de México.

Barkin, David. 1998. Mexican peasant strategies: Alternatives in the face of globalization. Paper presented at the XXI International Congress of the Latin American Studies Association, Chicago.

Barrera, Francisco, and Manuel Parra. 2000. El café en Chiapas y la investigación en ECOSUR [El Colegio de la Frontera Sur]. *ECOfronteras: Gaceta ECOSUR,* no. 12:3–6.

Barrera, Juan F., Francisco Infante, and Alfredo Castillo. 1996. *Control biológico para cafeticultores: La historieta como medio de diffusion de la ciencia y la tecnología.* Tapachula, Mexico: Colegio de la Frontera Sur.

Bartra, Armando. 1999. El aroma de la historia social del café. *La jornada del campo,* 28 Julio.

Bebbington, Anthony. 1997. Social capital and rural intensification: Local organizations and islands of sustainability in the rural Andes. *Geographical Journal* 163 (2): 189–97.

Benjamin, Craig. 1995. The Zapatista uprising and popular struggles against neo-liberal restructuring. *Labor, Capital, and Society* 27 (1): 109–28.

Black, Chad T. 1998. The 1990 Indian uprising in Ecuador: Culture ethnicity and post-Marxist social praxis. Paper presented at the XXI International Congress of the Latin American Studies Association, Chicago.

Borlaug, Norman. 1992. Small-scale agriculture in Africa: The myths and realities. *Feeding the Future,* no. 4:2.

———. 1994. Chemical fertilizer "essential." Letter to the editor. *International Agricultural Development* 23.

Boserup, Ester. 1965. *The conditions of agricultural growth: The economics of agrarian change under population pressure.* Chicago: Aldine.

Boyce, James K., and Manuel Pastor. 2001. Building natural assets: New strategies for poverty reduction and environmental protection. Research Report no. 3. Political Economy Research Institute and Center for Popular Economics, University of Massachusetts, Amherst.

Boyce, James K., and Barry G. Shelley. 2003. *Natural assets: Democratizing environmental ownership.* Boston: Island Press.

Bray, David. 1997. Conservación y desarrollo de las reservas de la biosfera y bosques communitarios en México. Paper presented at the XX International Congress of the Latin American Studies Association, Guadalajara.

Bray, D. B., L. Merino-Pérez, P. Negreros-Castillo, G. Segura-Warnholtz, J. Torres-Rojo, and H. Vester. 2003. Mexico's community-managed forests as a global model for sustainable landscapes. *Conservation Biology* 17 (3): 672–77.

Bretón Solo de Zaldívar, Victor. 2002. Cooperación al desarrollo, capital social y neo-indigenismo en los Andes ecuatorianos. *European Review of Latin American and Caribbean Studies,* no. 73:43–63.

Bryant, Raymond L., and Michael K. Goodman. 2004. Consuming narratives: The political ecology of "alternative" consumption. *Transactions of the Institute of British Geographers* 29 (3): 344–66.

Burbach, Roger, and Peter Rosset. 1994. *Chiapas and the crisis in Mexican agriculture.* USA: Food First Policy Brief No. 1.

Calva, José Luis. 1993. *La disputa por la tierra: La reforma del Artículo 27 y la nueva Ley Agraria.* Mexico City: Fontamara.

Carr, David L. 2000. Colonization, land use and deforestation in the Sierra de Lacandon National Park, Peter, Guatemala. Paper presented at the XXII International Congress of the Latin American Studies Association, Miami, Florida.

Carruthers, David V. 1995. Agroecology in Mexico: Linking environmental and indigenous struggles. Paper presented at the Conference on the Politics of Sustainable Agriculture, University of Oregon, Eugene.

Carruthers, I. 1993. Going, going, gone! Tropical agriculture as we knew it. *Tropical Agriculture Association Newsletter* 13 (3): 1–5.

Carvajal, José F. 1984. *Cafeto: Cultivo y fertilización.* 2d ed. Bern: Instituto Internacional de la Potasa.

Castells, Manuel. 1997. *The rise of the network society. The power of identity.* 2d ed. Oxford: Blackwell.

Catalán Tomás, Felipe. 1995. *La crisis de la producción del algodón y la expansión de la soya en la región del Soconusco, Chiapas, 1970–1988.* Mexico City: Centro de Investigaciones Humanisticas de Mesoamerica y del Estado de Chiapas, UNAM.

Caudillo Félix, Alicia Gloria. 1998. Los movimientos indígenas y la democracia: Un diálogo intercultural. Paper presented at the XXI International Congress of the Latin American Studies Association, Chicago.

CEC (Commission for Environmental Cooperation). 1999. Measuring consumer interest in Mexican shade-grown coffee: An assessment of the Canadian, Mexican, and U.S. markets. Montreal: CEC.

Celis, Fernando, Gabriela Ejea, and Luis Hernández Navarro. 1991. *Cafetaleros: La construcción de la autonomía.* Cuadernos Desarrollo de base, no. 3. Mexico City: Coordinadora Nacional de Organizaciones Cafetaleras.

Centro de Ecología. 1997. Deforestation, land use and development in the Greater Mayan Region. Mexico City: Global Ecology Laboratory, Centro de Ecología, UNAM.

Chapela Mendoza, Francisco. 1999. *Silvicultura comunitaria en la Sierra Norte de Oaxaca: El caso de la Unión Zapoteco-Chinanteca.* Mexico City: Red de Gestión de Recursos Naturales/Fundación Rockefeller.

Chayanov, A. V. 1986. *The theory of peasant economy.* Homewood, IL: American Economic Association.

Coleman, James. 1988. Social capital in the creation of human capital. *American Journal of Sociology* 94 (supplement): S95–120.

Collier, George. 1994. Background of the rebellion in Chiapas. Paper presented at the XVIII International Congress of the Latin American Studies Association, Atlanta.

———. 1996. Mexico: Restructuring ethnicity in Chiapas and the world. *Reconquista of identity. Indigenous struggle in the Americas.*

———. 1999. *Basta! Land and the Zapatista rebellion in Chiapas.* Oakland: Food First.

COPLADE (Comité de Planeación para el Desarrollo del Estado). 2000. Programa de desarrollo agropecuario, Chiapas, 1995–2000. COPLADE, Gobierno del Estado de Chiapas, Tuxtla Gutiérrez, 21–38.

Cortés Ruiz, Carlos. 1998. Hay futuro para la población de la Selva Lacandona? Colonización y desarrollo sustentable en Marqués de Comillas. Paper presented at the XXI International Congress of the Latin American Studies Association, Chicago.

Costanza, Robert, Ralph d'Arge, Rudolf de Groot, Stephen Ferber, Monica Grasso, Bruce Hannon, Karin Limburg, Shahid Naeem, Robert V. Oneill, Jose Paruelo, Robert G. Raskin, Paul Sutton, and Marjan van der Belt. 1997. The value of the world's ecosystem services and natural capital. *Nature* 387:253–59.

Craipeau, Carine. 1993. Actitudes diferenciadas de los pequeños productores en zonas cafetaleras marginales. Paper presented at the Simposio Latinoamericano de Modernización Tecnológica, Costa Rica.

Dardón, José A. 1995. *Memorias: Conferencia internacional sobre café orgánico.* Mexico City: IFOAM-AMAE-UACH.

Deinlein, Ronald. 1993. Algunos ejemplos del desarrollo de los suelos en diferentes niveles altitudinales en el Soconusco. In *Investigaciones eco-geográficas sobre la región del Soconusco, Chiapas,* ed. Michael Richter. Mexico City: Centro de Investigaciones Ecológicas del Sureste.

De Janvry, Alain, and Elisabeth Sadoulet. 2004. Toward a territorial approach to rural development: International experiences and implications for Mexico's Microregions Strategy. Working Paper, Agricultural and Resources Economics, University of California, Berkeley.

Dicum, Gregory, and Nina Luttinger. 1999. *The coffee book: Anatomy of an industry from crop to the last drop.* Bazaar Books, no. 2. New York: New Press.

DowElanco. 1994. *The Bottom Line.* Indianapolis: DowElanco.

ECOSUR (El Colegio de la Frontera Sur). 1995. Organizaciones de la sociedad civil en Chiapas. Report to the Interamerican Development Bank.

EFTA (European Fair Trade Association). 1998. *Annual report.* Amsterdam: EFTA.

Ellis, Frank. 1988. *Peasant economics: Farm households and agrarian development.* Cambridge: Cambridge University Press.

Embamex (Embajada de México). 1999. *Situación y perspectivas de nuestra region fronteriza.* Guatemala City: Embajada de México en Guatemala.

Enríquez, Laura. 1997. *Agrarian reform and class consciousness in Nicaragua.* Gainesville: University Press of Florida.

Escamilla Prado, Esteban. 1993. *El café cereza en México: Tecnología de la producción.* Texcoco: Universidad Autónoma Chapingo, Centro de Investigaciones Económicas, Sociales y Tecnológicas de la Agroindustria y de la Agricultura Mundial (CIESTAAM), Dirección de Centros Regionales.

Evans, Peter. 1996a. Government action, social capital and development: Reviewing the evidence on synergy. *World Development* 24 (6): 1119–32.

———. 1996b. *State-society synergy: Government and social capital in development.* Berkeley: Institute for International Studies, University of California.

FNC (Federación Nacional de Cafeteros de Colombia), 2005. Información economía cafetera: Producción mundial total de café verde: Años cosecha 1999/2000–2003/4. Retrieved at http://www.cafedecolombia.com.

Foley, Michael W. 1991. Agenda for mobilization: The agrarian question and popular mobilization in contemporary Mexico. *Latin America Research Review* 26 (2): 39–74.

Fox, Jonathan. 1993. *The politics of food in Mexico: State power and social mobilization.* Ithaca: Cornell University Press.

———. 1994. Political change in Mexico's new peasant economy. In *The politics of economic restructuring: State-society relations.* San Diego: Center for U.S.-Mexican Studies.

———. 1996. How does civil society thicken? The political construction of social capital in rural Mexico. *World Development* 24 (6): 1089–2004.

———. 1997. The World Bank and social capital: Contesting the concept. *Journal of International Development* 9 (7): 963–71.

Freyermuth, Graciela, and Nancy Godfrey. 1993. *Refugiados guatemaltecos en México: La vida en continuo estado de emergencia.* Mexico City: CIESAS and Instituto Chiapaneco de Cultura.

García, Arturo. 1991. Proceso de construcción del movimiento campesino en México: La experiencia de la CNOC. In *Cafetaleros: La construcción de la autonomía,* ed. Fernando Celis, Gabriela Ejea, Luis Hernández Navarro. Cuadernos desarrollo de base, no. 3. Mexico City: Coordinadora Nacional de Organizaciones Cafetaleras.

García, Enriqueta. 1982. *Modificaciones al sistema de clasificación climática de Köppen adaptada a México.* Mexico City: UNAM.

García de León, Antonio. 1985. *Resistencia y utopia: Memorial de agravios y crónicas de revueltas y profecías acaecidas en la Provincia de Chiapas durante los ultimos quinientos años de su historia.* Mexico City: Ediciones Era.

Garza Caligaris, Anna María, María Fernanda Paz Salinas, Juana María Ruiz Ortiz, and Angelino Calvo Sánchez. 1993. *Sk'op Antzetik: Una historia de mujeres en la selva de Chiapas.* Tuxtla Gutiérrez, Chiapas: Universidad Autónoma de Chiapas.

Geertz, Clifford. 1963. *Agricultural involution: The process of ecological change in Indonesia.* Berkeley: University of California Press.

Gittell, Ross, and Avis Vidal. 1998. *Community organizing: Building social capital as a development strategy.* Newbury Park, CA: Sage Publications.

González, Alma Amalia, Thierry Linck, and Reyna Moguel. 2003. El comercio de valores éticos: Las reglas del juego del café solidario. *Revista europea de estudios latinoamericanos y del Caribe* 75:31–45.

González, Alma Amalia, and Ronald Nigh. 2004. Who says it's organic? Certification and smallholder participation in the global market. Paper prepared for the 10th Biennial Meeting of the International Association for the Study of Common Property, 9–13 August, 2004, Oaxaca.

González Ponciano, Jorge Ramon. 1995. Marques de Comillas: Cultura y sociedad en la Selva Fronterize Mexico-Guatemala. In *Chiapas: Los rumbo de otra historia,* edited by Juan Pedro Viqueira and Mario Humberto Ruz. Mexico City: Centro de Estudios Mayas del Instituto de Investigaciones Filológicas y Coordinación de Humanidades UNAM, CIESAS, Centro de Estudios Mexicanos y Centroamericanos and Universidad de Gudalajara.

Goodman, M. 2004. Reading fair trade: Political ecological imaginary and the moral economy of fair trade foods. *Political Geography* 23 (7): 891–915.

Gorman, Laura. 1999. Major specialty coffee-producing country of origin guide. *Gourmet Retailer,* March: 110–29.

Granovetter, Mark S. 1973. The strength of the weak ties. *American Journal of Sociology* 78 (6): 1360–80.

Greenberg, Russell. 1996. Birds in the tropics: The coffee connection. *Birding.*

———. 2001. Criteria working group thought paper. Washington, DC: Smithsonian Migratory Bird Center.

Greenberg, Russell, Peter Bichier, Andrea Cruz Angón, and Robert Reitsma. 1997. Bird populations in shade and sun coffee plantations in central Guatemala. *Conservation Biology* 11 (2): 448–59.

Greenfield, Mirna. 1994. Alternative trade: Giving coffee a new flavor. In *Making coffee strong.* Boston: Equal Exchange.

Gupta, Anil. 1996. Social and ethical dimensions of ecological economics. In *Getting down to earth: Practical applications of ecological economics,* ed. Robert Costanza, Olman Segura Bonilla, and Juan Martínez Alier. Washington, DC: Island Press.

Harriss, John, and Paolo De Renzio. 1997. "Missing link" or analytically missing: The concept of social capital: An introductory bibliographic essay. *Journal of International Development* 9 (7): 919–38.

Hart, Mónica de. 1997. Decolonizing reality: Ethnic development organizations in Guatemala and Mexico. Paper presented at the XX International Congress of the Latin American Studies Association, Guadalajara.

Harvey, Neil. 1994. *Rebellion in Chiapas: Rural reforms, campesino radicalism, and the limits to Salinismo.* Transformation of Rural Mexico, no 5. San Diego, Center for U.S.-Mexican Studies, University of California, San Diego.

———. 1998. El neoliberalismo y nuevas periferias rurales en México: El caso de la zona de Marqués de Comillas, Chiapas. Paper presented at the XXI International Congress of the Latin American Studies Association, Chicago.

Hazell, Peter. 1995. *Managing agricultural intensification.* 20/20 Brief no. 11. Washington, DC: IFPRI.

Heinegg, Ayo, and Karen M. Ferroggiaro. 1996. Inter-American foundation strategy in the Mexican coffee sector: A case study of ISMAM. Paper. Chiapas.

Helbig, Carlos. 1964. *El Soconusco y su zona cafetalera en Chiapas.* Mexico City: Instituto de Ciencias y Artes de Chiapas.

———. 1976. *Chiapas: Geografía de un estado mexicano.* Tuxtla Gutiérrez, Chiapas: UNACH, Gobierno del Estado de Chiapas.

Hernández, Luis. 1991. Nadando con los tiburones: La Coordinadora Nacional de Organizaciones Cafetaleras. In *Cafetaleros: La construcción de la autonomía,* ed. Fernando Celis, Gabriela Ejea, and Luis Hernández. Cuadernos de desarrollo de base, no. 3. Mexico City: CNOC.

Hernández Castillo, Rosalva Aida, and Ronald Nigh. 1998. Global processes and local identity among Mayan coffee growers in Chiapas, Mexico. *American Anthropologist* 100 (1): 136–47.

Hewitt, Tracy I., and Katie R. Smith. 1995. *Intensive agriculture and environmental quality: Examining the newest agricultural myth.* Greenbelt, MD: Henry Wallace Institute for Alternative Agriculture.

Hinterberger, Friedrich, Fred Luks, and Friedrich Schmidt-Bleek. 1997. Material flows vs. "natural capital": What makes an economy sustainable? *Ecological Economics* 23 (1): 1–14.

Howard, Philip. 1995. Environmental scarcities and conflict in Chiapas: The impoverishing chain of resource capture and ecological marginalization. Paper for the Fast Track Project on Environment, Population and Security, University College, Peace and Conflict Studies Department.

ICO (International Coffee Organization). 2003. Share of the markets in each group of coffee and their weighting in the calculation of the ICO composite indicator price, from 1 October 2003. ICO document EB-3776/01, annex 1.

———. 2005a Averages of the ICO composite indicator price. Retrieved at http://www.ico.org/asp/display10.asp.

———. 2005b. Documents available at www.ico.org/electdocs/archives/cy2003–04/Spanish/edletter/nov03.pdf.

———. 2005c. Total production of exporting countries, crop years 1999/00 to 2004/05. Retrieved at http://www.ico.org/prices/po.htm.

IFOAM (International Federation of Organic Agriculture Movements). 1995. Basic standards for organic agriculture and food processing.

Jaffee D., J. Kloppenburg Jr., and M. B. Monroy. 2004. Bringing the "moral charge" home? Fair trade within the north and within the south. *Rural Sociology* 69 (2): 1169–96.

Jansson, AnnMari, Monica Hammer, Carl Folke, and Robert Costanza, eds. 1994. *Investing in natural capital: The ecological economics approach to sustainability.* Washington, DC: Island Press.

Junguito Bonnet, Roberto, and Diego Pizano Salazar. 1993. *El comercio exterior y la política internacional del café.* Santafé de Bogotá: Fedesarrollo/Fondo Cultural Cafetero.

Kleinbaum, David G., Lawrence L. Kupper, Keith E. Muller, and Azhar Nizam. 1998. *Applied regression analysis and other multivariable methods.* London: Duxbury Press.

Knutson, Ronald D., J. B. Taylor, J. B. Benson, and E. G. Smith. 1990. *Economic impacts of reduced chemical use.* College Station: Texas A&M University.

Köhler, Urlich. 2000. The Mayans of Chiapas since 1965. Supplement to *Handbook of Middle American Indians. Ethnology* 6:179–206.

Krivonos, Ekaterina. 2004. The impact of the coffee market reforms on producer prices and price transmission. World Bank Policy Research Working Paper no. 3358, July 2004.

Landazuri Benites, Gisela. 1997. Encuentros y desencuentros entre campesinos y asesores en el medio rural: El caso de Cuentepec, Morelos. Paper presented at the XX International Congress of the Latin American Studies Association, Guadalajara.

Lazos Chavero, Elena. 1996. La ganaderización de dos comunidades veracruzanas: Condiciones de la diffusion de un modelo agrario. In *El ropaje de la tierra: Naturaleza y cultura en cinco zonas rurales,* ed. L. Paré and M. J. Sánchez. Mexico City: UNAM/Plaza y Valdés.

Leff, Enrique. 1996. From ecological economics to productive ecology: Perspectives on sustainable development from the south. In *Getting down to earth: Practical applications of ecological economics,* ed. Robert Costanza, Olman Segura, and Juan Martínez Alier. Washington, DC: Island Press.

Lele, Sharachandra M. 1991. Sustainable development: A critical review. *World Development* 19 (6): 607–21.

Lombana Mejía, Pedro Manuel. 1991. *Café año 2000: Investigación acerca de los efectos del rompimiento del pacto de cuotas del Convenio Internacional del Café.* Manizales, Colombia: Editorial Papiro.

López Meza, Antonio. 1996. Organización tradicional y asociación de productores en Tenejapa, Chiapas. Master's thesis, Autonomous University of Chapingo, Regional Rural Development Program.

Majomut (Unión de Ejidos Majomut). 1996. *Reglamento interno de producción de café orgánico para productores de la Unión Majomut.* Chiapas: Unión de Ejidos Majomut.

Marquez Rosano, Conrado. 1990. Evolución del patron de uso de suelo en la subregión de las Cañadas de la Selva Lacandona. *Revista de Difusion Científica, Tecnológica y Humanística,* no. 2:19–24.

Martínez, Eduardo, and Walter Peters. 1991. El sistema agroforestal de la Finca Irlanda: Descripción y actividades. Technical report. Tapachula, Mexico.

———. 1994. Cafeticultura ecológica en el estado de Chiapas: Un estudio de caso. Study. Tapachula, Mexico.

———. 1995. Cafeticultura orgánico-biodinámico en la Sierra Madre de Chiapas, 1963–1993. Paper presented at Conferencia Internacional sobre Café Orgánico: Memorias, Chapingo, Mexico.

Martínez Alier, Juan. 1995. The environment as a luxury good, or Too poor to be green. *Ecological Economics* 13:1–10.

Martínez Alier, Juan, and Martin O'Connor. 1996. Distributional issues in ecological economics. In *Getting down to earth: Practical applications of ecological economics,* ed. Robert Costanza, Olman Segura, and Juan Martínez-Alier, 153–84. Washington, DC: Island Press.

Martínez Borrego, Estela. 1991. *Organización de productores y movimiento campesino.* Mexico City: Siglo XXI.

Martínez Morales, Aurora Cristina. 1997. *El proceso cafetalero mexicano.* 1st ed. Mexico City: Instituto de Investigaciones Económicas, UNAM.

Martínez Quezada, A. 1990. Cafeticultura y política neoliberal en los altos de Chiapas. In *Los altos de Chiapas: Agricultura y crisis rural,* ed. Manuel R. Parra Vázquez and Blanca M. Díaz Hernández. Vol. 2, *Los sistemas de producción agropecuaria.* Chiapas: El Colegio de la Frontera Sur.

Martínez-Torres, Maria Elena. 2001. Civil society, the Internet, and the Zapatista movement. *Peace Review* 13 (3): 347–55.

———. 2003. Sustainable development, campesino organizations, and technological change among small coffee producers in Chiapas, Mexico. PhD diss., University of California, Berkeley.

——. 2004 "Survival strategies in neoliberal markets: peasant organizations and organic coffee in Chiapas." in *Challenging neoliberal globalism: Mexico in Transition?* ed. Gerardo Otero, 169–85. London: Zed Books.

Mas, Alexandre H., and Thomas V. Dietsch. 2000. Evaluating shade coffee certification programs: A case study using butterfly diversity in Chiapas, Mexico. Paper presented at the XXII International Congress of the Latin American Studies Association, Miami.

Masera, Omar R., Martha Astier, and Ruben Puentes. Compendio sobre evaluación de proyectos e indicadores de sustentabilidad. 1995. Working paper no. 12, Grupo Interdisciplinario de Tecnología Apropiada. Mexico City.

Meda, Dahinda. 1995. From cultural survival and liberation theology to medflies and political assassinations: A study of the ISMAM cooperative of Chiapas, Mexico. Paper presented at the Politics of Sustainable Agriculture conference, University of Oregon, Eugene.

Mera Ovando, Luz María. 1989. Condiciones naturales para la producción. In *El subdesarrollo agrícola en los altos de Chiapas,* ed. Manuel Roberto Parra Vázquez. Colección cuadernos universitarios, serie agronomía, no. 18. Texcoco, Mexico: Universidad Autonoma de Chapingo/Centro de Investigaciones Ecológicas del Sureste.

Mogues, Tewodaj, and Michael R. Carter. 2004. Social capital and the reproduction of inequality in socially polarized economies. University of Wisconsin Working Paper.

Monzote, Marta, Eulogio Muñoz, and Fernando Funes-Monzote. 2002. The integration of crops and livestock. In *Sustainable agriculture and resistance: Transforming food production in Cuba,* ed. Fernando Funes, Luis García, Martín Bourque, Nilda Pérez, and Peter Rosset, 190–212. Oakland: Food First.

Moscoso Pastrana, Prudencio. 1992. Rebeliones indígenas en los Altos de Chiapas. Mexico: UNAM, Centro de Investigaciones Humanísticas de Mesoamerica y del Estado de Chiapas.

Murray, Douglas L., and Laura T. Raynolds, 1998. Yes, we have no bananas: Re-regulating global and regional trade. *International Journal of Sociology of Agriculture and Food* 7:7–44

——. 2000. Alternative trade in bananas: Obstacles and opportunities for progressive social change in the global economy. *Agriculture and Human Values* 17:65–74.

Nestel, D., and M. A. Altieri. 1992. The weed community of Mexican coffee agroecosystems: Effect of management upon plant biomass and species composition. *Acta oecologia* 13:715–26.

Nigh, Ronald. 1991. Associative corporations, organic agriculture, and peasant strategies in post-modern Mexico. Paper presented at the XVI International Congress of the Latin American Studies Association, Washington, DC.

———. 1997. Organic agriculture and globalization: A Maya associative corporation in Chiapas, Mexico. *Human Organization* 56 (4): 427–36.

———. 2002. Acción colectiva, capital social y recursos naturales: Las organizaciones agroecológicas de Chiapas. In *De lo privado a lo pública: Organizaciones en Chiapas,* ed. G. Vargas, 73–110. Mexico City: Porrúa/CIESAS.

Nolasco, Margarita. 1985. *Café y sociedad en México.* 1st ed. Mexico City: Centro de Ecodesarrollo.

North, Douglas. 1990. *Institutions, institutional change, and economic performance.* Cambridge: Cambridge University Press.

O'Connor, Martin. 1994. El mercadeo de la naturaleza: Sobre los infortunios de la naturaleza capitalista. *Ecología política,* no. 7.

Odile, Marie, and Marion Singer. 1983. *El movimiento campesino en Chiapas, 1983.* Mexico City: Centro de Estudios Historicos del Agrarismo en México (CEHAM).

Ostrom, Elinor. 1996. Crossing the great divide: Coproduction, synergy and development. *World Development* 24 (6): 1073–87.

Otero, Gerardo. 2004. *Challenging neoliberal globalism: Mexico in transition?* London: Zed Books.

Paarlberg, R. L. 1994. *Sustainable farming: A political geography.* 2020 Briefs. Washington, DC: *IFPRI.*

Paige, Jeffery M. 1998. *Coffee and power: Revolution and the rise of democracy in Central America.* 2d ed. Cambridge, MA: Harvard University Press.

Parra, Manuel, and Reyna Moguel. 1995. La tierra: Necesaria pero no suficiente. Working paper, El Colegio de la Frontera Sur, Chiapas.

Parra, Victor, and Reyna Moguel. 1996. Emergencia de ONG's de cafeticultores indígenas en Chiapas: Estrategias frente a las políticas agrícolas. San Cristóbal de las Casas, Chiapas.

Parra Vázquez, Manuel Roberto. 1989. *El subdesarrollo agrícola en los altos de Chiapas.* Mexico City: UACH/CIES.

Parra Vázquez, Manuel R., and Blanca M. Díaz Hernández. 1997. *Los altos de Chiapas: Agricultura y crisis rural.* Vol. 1, *Los recursos naturales.* Mexico City: ECOSUR.

Pastor, Manuel. 2001. *Building social capital to protect natural capital: The quest for environmental justice.* Working Papers, Political Economy Research Institute, University of Massachusetts, Amherst.

Pearce, David, and R. Kerry Turner. 1990. *Economics of natural resources and the environment.* Baltimore: Johns Hopkins University Press.

Pendergrast, Mark. 1999. *Uncommon grounds: The history of coffee and how it transformed our world.* New York: Basic Books.

Peña, Guillermo de la. 1998. Etnicidad, ciudadanía y cambio agrario: Apuntes comparativos sobre tres paises latinoamericanos. In *Las disputas por el México rural: Transformacions de prácticas, identidades y proyectos,* ed. Sergio Zendejas and Peter de Vries, 2:67–98. Zamora: El Colegio de Michoacán.

Pérez Brignoli, Héctor, and Mario Samper. 1994. *Tierra, café y sociedad.* Mexico City: FLACSO.

Pérez Castro, Ana Bella. 1989. *Entre montañas y cafetales: Luchas agrarias en el norte de Chiapas.* Mexico City: UNAM.

Perezgrovas Garza, Victor. 1996. Evaluación de la sustentabilidad del sistema de producción de café orgánico en la Unión Majomut, en la región de los Altos de Chiapas. Master's thesis, University of Chapingo, Mexico.

Perezgrovas Garza, Victor, Edith Cervantes, and John Burstein. 2001. Case study of the coffee sector in Mexico. Oxford: Oxfam.

Perezgrovas Garza, Victor, Marvey López Vences, Walter Anzueto, Fernando Rodríguez López, and Eliseo Gómez Hernández. 1997. *El cultivo del café orgánico en la Unión Majomut: Un proceso de rescate, sistematización, evaluación y divulgación de tecnología agrícola.* Serie estudios de caso sobre participación campesina en generación, validación y transferencia de tecnología. Mexico City: Red de Gestión de Recursos Naturales/ Fundación Rockefeller.

Perfecto, Ivette, Robert Rice, Russell Greenberg, and Martha E. Van der Voort. 1996. Shade coffee: A disappearing refuge for biodiversity. Draft report, School of Natural Resources, University of Michigan.

Perfecto, Ivette, and John Vandermeer. 1994. Understanding biodiversity loss in agroecosystems: Reduction of ant diversity resulting from transformation of the coffee ecosystem in Costa Rica. *Entomology Trends in Agriculture,* no. 2:7–13.

Plaza Sánchez, José Luis. 1997. Conservación y desarrollo sostenido: La producción de café orgánico en Las Margaritas, Chiapas. In *Semillas para el cambio en el campo: Medio ambiente, mercados y organización campesina,* ed. Luisa Paré, David B. Bray, John Burstein, and Sergio Martínez Vásquez. Mexico: UNAM.

Plaza Sánchez, José Luis, Ellen Contreras Murphy, and David Bray Barton. 1998. A basket of benefits: Ecosystems, economics and organizations in the production of organic coffee in Chiapas, Mexico. Paper presented at the XXI International Congress of the Latin American Studies Association, Chicago.

Pohlenz Córdova, Juan. 1995. *Dependencia y desarrollo capitalista en la sierra de Chiapas.* 1st ed. Chiapas: UNAM/Centro de Investigaciones Humanísticas de Mesoamérica.

Portes, Alejandro. 1998. Social capital: Its origins and applications in modern sociology. *Annual Review of Sociology* 22:1–24.

Portes, Alejandro, and Patricia Landolt. 1996. The downside of social capital. *American Prospect* 26:18–21.

Posada, Marcelo, and Irene Velarde. 2000. Estrategias de desarrollo local a partir de productos alimenticios típicos: El caso del vino de la costa en Buenos Aires, Argentina. *Revista problemas del desarrollo* 31 (121): 63–85.

Pretty, Jules. 1995a. Participatory learning for sustainable agriculture. *World Development* 23 (8): 1247–63.

———. 1995b. *Regenerating agriculture: Policies and practices for sustainability and self-reliance.* 1st ed. London: Earthscan.

———. 1997. The sustainable intensification of agriculture. *Natural Resources Forum* 21 (4): 247–56.

———. 1998. Sustainable agricultural intensification: Farmer participation, social capital, and technology design. Paper prepared for the World Bank's Rural Week, Washington, DC.

———. 1999. Current challenges for agricultural development. Paper presented at the Kentucky Cooperative Extension Service Conference, January 13–15, Lexington.

———. 2003. Social capital and the collective management of resources. *Science* 302:1912–14.

Pretty, Jules, and R. Hine. 2001. *Reducing food poverty with sustainable agriculture: A summary of new evidence.* Centre for Environment and Society, University of Essex.

Pretty, Jules, J. I. L. Morison, and R. E. Hine. 2003. Reducing food poverty by increasing agricultural sustainability in developing countries. *Agriculture, Ecosystems and Environment* 95 (1): 217–34.

Pretty, Jules, and H. Ward. 2001. Social capital and the environment. *World Development* 29 (2): 209–27.

Prugh, Thomas, Robert Costanza, John H. Cumberland, Herman E. Daly, Robert Goodland, and Richard B. Norgaard. 1999. *Natural capital and human economic survival.* 2d ed. Ecological Economics Series. London: Lewis Publishers; New York: International Society for Ecological Economics.

Putnam, Robert, with Robert Leonardi and Raffaella Nanetti. 1993. *Making democracy work: Civic traditions in modern Italy.* Princeton: Princeton University Press.

Quiroga Martínez, Rayen. 1999. El capital natural en el desarrollo de la sustentabilidad. Paper. University of Chile.

Raynolds, Laura T. 2000. Re-embedding global agriculture: The international organic and fair trade movements. *Agriculture and Human Values* 17:297–309.

RBO (Royal Blue Organics). Café Mam: Know Beans! 1994. Eugene: RBO.

Reijntjes, Coen, Bertus Haverkort, and Ann Waters-Bayer. 1996. *Farming for the future: An introduction to low-external-input and sustainable agriculture.* London: Macmillan.

Rello, Fernando. 2000. Estrategias campesinas frente al ajuste y la globalización en México. *Investigación económica* 60 (233): 61–76.

Renard, María Cristina. 1993. *El Soconusco: Una economía cafetalera.* 1st ed. Texcoco, Mexico: Universidad Autonoma de Chapingo.

———. 1999. *Los intersticios de la globalización: Un label (Max Havelaar) para los pequeños productores de café.* Mexico City: Centre Français d'Études Mexicaines et Centraméricaines.

Restrepo Salazar, Juan Camilo. 1990. *Ensayos de política económica cafetera.* Bogotá: Editorial Presencia.

Rice, Paul D., and Jennifer McLean. 1999. *Sustainable coffee at the crossroads.* Washington, DC: Consumer's Choice Council.

Rice, Robert A. 1993. New technology in coffee production: Examining landscape transformation and international aid in northern Latin America. Paper. Washington, DC: Smithsonian Migratory Bird Center.

———. 1997. Land use patterns and the history of coffee in eastern Chiapas, Mexico. *Agricultural and Human Values* 14:127–43.

——. 1999. A place unbecoming: The coffee farm of northern Latin America. *Geographical Review* 89 (4): 554–579.

——. 2000. Managed biodiversity in shade coffee systems: The non-coffee harvest. Paper presented at the XXII International Congress of the Latin American Studies Association, Miami.

——. 2003. Coffee production in a time of crisis: Social and environmnetal connections. *SAIS Review* 23 (1): 221–45.

Rice, Robert A., and Justin R. Ward. 1996. *Coffee, conservation, and commerce in the Western Hemisphere*. New York: Natural Resource Defense Council; Washington, DC: Smithsonian Migratory Bird Center.

——. 1997. From shade to sun: The industrialization of coffee production. *Global Pesticide Campaigner* 7 (3).

Richter, Michael. 1993. Ecological effects of inappropriate cultivation methods at different altitudes in the Soconusco Region/southern Mexico. *Plant Research and Development* 37:19–44.

Robles Guadarrama, Carlos Augusto, and Elsa Almeida Monterde. 1998. *Experimentación campesina y tecnológica sustentable en Los Tuxtlas: El camino hacia una agricultura ecológica*. Mexico City: Red de gestión de Recursos Naturales/Fundación Rockefeller.

Romero, Matías. 1893. *Cultivo del café en la costa meridional de Chiapas*. Mexico City: Secretaría de Fomento.

Roseberry, William, Lowell Gudmundson, and Mario Samper Kutschbach. 1995. *Coffee, society, and power in Latin America*. Johns Hopkins Studies in Atlantic History and Culture. Baltimore: Johns Hopkins University Press.

Rosset, Peter. 1999. The multiple functions and benefits of small farm agriculture in the context of global trade. Food First Policy Brief no. 4, Institute for Food and Development Policy, Oakland.

——. 2001. Access to land: Land reform and security of tenure: Case study of the civil society input for the World Food Summit/Five years later. Rome: FAO.

Rosset, Peter M., and Miguel A. Altieri. 1997. Agroecology vs. input substitution: A fundamental contradiction of sustainable agriculture. *Sociology and Natural Resources* 10 (3): 283–95.

Salazar Peralta, Ana María. 1993. *La política neoliberal y el café en México*. Mexico City: IIA/UNAM.

Samper K., Mario. 1994. Los paisajes sociales del café: Reflexiones compara-
das. In *Tierra, café y sociedad*, ed. Héctor Pérez Brignoli and Mario Samper, 9–54. Costa Rica: FLACSO.

Sánchez López, Roberto. 1990. *El cultivo biológico del café orgánico.* Motozintla, Mexico: ISMAM.

Santoyo Cortes, V. Horacio, Salvador Díaz Cardenas, and Benigno Rodríguez
Padrón. 1996. *Sistema agroindustrial del café en México: Diagnóstico,
problemática y alternativas.* Mexico City: Universidad Autonoma de
Chapingo/CIESTAAM.

SCAA (Specialty Coffee Association of America). 2003. Annual report. Long
Beach, CA: SCAA.

Schumacher, E. F. 1983. *Lo pequeño es hermoso.* Barcelona: Ediciones Orbis.

Schumann, Otto. 1969. El Tuzanteco y su posición dentro de las lenguas de la
familia Maya. *Anales del Instituto Nacional de Antropología e Historia
(1967–68)* 1 (49): 139–48.

Seggern, Jorg v. 1993. Algunas observaciones sobre la erosión del suelo en el
Soconusco. In *Investigaciones ecogeográficas sobre la región del Soconusco, Chiapas,* ed. Michael Richter. Chiapas: Centro de Investigaciones Ecológicas del Sureste.

Selna, Robert. 1999. Berkeley mayor wants city to buy only organic coffee.
San Francisco Examiner, June 8, A-7.

Sick, Deborah. 1999. *Farmers of the golden bean: Costa Rican households and
the global coffee economy.* DeKalb: Northern Illinois University Press.

Simpson, Charles, and Anita Rapone. 1998. Community development from
the ground up: Community-based production and social justice marketing of coffee. (Manuscript.) State University of New York, Plattsburgh.

———. Community development from the ground up: Social-justice coffee.
Human Ecology Review 7 (1): 46–57.

Skocpol, Theda. 1995. *Social policy in the United States: Future possibilities
in historical perspective.* Princeton: Princeton University Press.

Soto, Lorena. 2001. Características ecológicas que influyen en la producción
de café. PhD diss., Colegio de la Frontera Sur, Chiapas.

Steer, A., and E. Lutz. 1993. Measuring environmentally sustainable development. *Finance and Development* 30 (2): 20–23.

Taller de Análisis de las Cuestiones Agrarias. 1988. *Los zapatistas de Chiapas.*
San Cristóbal de Las Casas, Chiapas: Taller de Análisis de las Cuestiones
Agrarias.

Tarrow, Sidney. 1994. *Power in movement: Social movements, collective action, and politics.* Cambridge: Cambridge University Press.

——. 1996. Making social science work across space and time: A critical reflection on Robert Putnam's *Making democracy work. American Political Science Review* 90 (2): 389–97.

Tendler, Judith. 1995. Social capital and the public sector: The blurred boundaries between private and public. Paper. Department of Urban Studies and Planning, MIT.

——. 1997. *Good government in the tropics.* Baltimore: John Hopkins University Press.

Thrupp, Lori Ann. 1997. Nuevas oportunidades de mercado para el café orgánico. Paper presented at Taller de CATIE-IICA sobre Políticas de Plaguicidas en América Central. Turrialba, Costa Rica.

Toledo, V. M., B. Ortiz-Espejel, L. Cortés, P. Moguel, and M. D. J. Ordoñez. 2003. The multiple use of tropical forests by indigenous peoples in Mexico: A case of adaptive management. *Conservation Ecology* 7 (3): 9.

Toledo, Victor M., Ana I. Batis, Rosalba Becerra, Esteban Martinez, and Clara Ramos. 1995. La selva útil: Etnobotánica cuantitativa de los grupos indígenas del trópico húmedo de México. *Interciencia* 20 (4): 177–87.

TransFair USA. 2005. FastFact: Fair trade certified coffee. Retrieved at http://www.transfairusa.org/pdfs/fastfacts_coffe.pdf.

Ukers, William H. 1935. *All about coffee.* New York: Tea and Coffee Trade Journal Company.

UN (United Nations). UNCTAD Secretariat. 1984. The processing and marketing of coffee: Areas for international co-operation. Studies in the processing, marketing and distribution of commodities, TD/B/C.1/PSC/31/Rev.1. New York: United Nations.

UNDP (United Nations Development Programme). 1995. Agroecology: Creating the synergism for a sustainable agriculture. Guidebook Series. New York: UNDP.

USDA (United States Department of Agriculture). 2005. Foreign Agricultural Service, Bico import commodity aggregations. Retrieved at http://www.fas.usda.gov/ustrade.

Velasco Palacios, Antonio. 1988. *Historia de Chiapas.* Chiapas: Impresora Marina.

Viederman, S. 1994. Ecological literacy: Can colleges save the world? Paper. Associated Colleges of the Midwest Conference on Ecological Education, Beloit College.

Villafuerte Solis, Daniel, and Salvador Meza Díaz. 1993. Los productores de café del Soconusco. In *El café en la frontera sur: La producción y los productores del Soconusco, Chiapas,* ed. Daniel Villafuerte. Nuestros Pueblos. Mexico: Instituto Chiapaneco de Cultura.

von Amsberg, Joachim. 2001. *Project evaluation and the depletion of natural capital: An application of the sustainability principle.* Washington, DC: World Bank, Environment Department.

Voorhies, Barbara. 1991. *La economía del antiguo Soconusco, Chiapas.* Mexico City: UNAM.

Vos, Jan de. 1980. *La paz de Dios y del rey: La conquista de la Selva Lacandona, 1521–1821.* Mexico City: Fondo de Cultura Económica.

———. 2002. *Una tierra para sembrar sueños: Historia reciente de la Selva Lacandona, 1950–2000.* Mexico City: CIESAS/Fondo de Cultura Económica.

Wackernagel, Mathis, and William E. Rees. 1997. Perceptual and structural barriers to investing in natural capital: Economics from an ecological footprint perspective. *Ecological Economics,* no. 20.

Williams, Robert G. 1994. *States and social evolution: Coffee and the rise of national governments in Central America.* Chapel Hill: University of North Carolina Press.

Winters, Paul, Leonardo Corral, and Gustavo Gordillo. 2001. Rural livelihood strategies and social capital in Latin America: Implications for rural development projects. University of New England, Working Paper Series in Agricultural and Resource Economics, no. 2001–6.

Wohlgemuth, Neusa Hidalgo-Monroy. 1996. Organic agriculture and indigenous communities in Chiapas, Mexico: An alternative to rural development. PhD diss., University of California, Berkeley.

Wolf, Eric R. 1982. *Europe and the people without history.* Berkeley: University of California Press.

Wood, W. Warner. 2000. Flexible production, households, and fieldwork: Multisided Zapotec weavers in the era of late capitalism. *Ethnology* 39 (2): 133–48.

Woolcock, Michael, and Deepa Narayan. 2000. Social capital: Implications for development theory, research, and policy. *World Bank Research Observer* 15 (2): 225–49.

World Bank. 1997. The initiative on defining, monitoring and measuring social capital. Social Capital Initiative Working Paper no. 1, World Bank, Washington, DC.

Index

9 780896 802476